ZERO TRUST

Redefining Security in a Perimeterless WorldBill Johns

Bill Johns

Peninsula Network Security, LLC

2025

DEDICATION

To all my clients—past, present, and future—and to every cybersecurity professional who stands on the front lines, defending our digital world with courage and ingenuity. This book is dedicated to those who have entrusted us with their most critical systems, challenging us to innovate, adapt, and never settle for "good enough." Your unwavering faith and tireless commitment to safeguarding our digital infrastructure have not only shaped the way we think about security but have also inspired every chapter of this work.

I recall a client once told me, "*The adversary has to be right one time, and we have to be right every time.*" That single piece of advice encapsulates the high stakes of our mission—it is a constant reminder that every decision, every protocol, and every line of code must be crafted with precision and care.

This dedication honors that relentless pursuit of perfection and the deep trust placed in us by those we serve. May these pages inspire you to uphold the highest standards of security and to meet every challenge with unwavering resolve.

—Bill Johns

TABLE OF CONTENTS

Foreword

Introduction

Chapter 1: The Foundations of Zero Trust

Chapter 2: Zero Trust Architecture

Chapter 3: Planning and Strategy for Zero Trust Adoption

Chapter 4: Implementing Zero Trust – Practical Approaches

Chapter 5: Technologies and Tools for Zero Trust

Chapter 6: Zero Trust Case Studies and Real-World Applications

Chapter 7: Zero Trust in the Era of Remote Work and IoT

Chapter 8: Zero Trust for Cloud and Hybrid Environments

Chapter 9: Zero Trust and DevSecOps Integration

Chapter 10: Zero Trust for Small and Medium Enterprises

Chapter 11: Legal, Regulatory, and Ethical Considerations in Zero Trust

Chapter 12: Zero Trust Metrics, KPIs, and Continuous Improvement

Chapter 13: Building a Zero Trust Security Culture

Chapter 14: The Zero Trust Vendor Ecosystem and Future Trends

Chapter 15: Conclusion – The Path Forward in a Zero Trust World

About the Author

FOREWORD

I still remember the early days of networking, when the idea of protecting data felt almost tangible—you could see and touch the systems you were defending. Back then, networks were isolated islands of computers, all housed within the same building or even the same room. Security was simple; you built a strong wall around your systems, locked the doors, and trusted that everything inside was safe. I worked on mainframes and early local area networks, and the concept of cyber threats was almost unimaginable. We had physical security measures that you could visually inspect, and it was enough to simply secure the perimeter because the world outside rarely intruded.

As the digital revolution unfolded, we witnessed a profound transformation. With the advent of the internet, connectivity broke down those once-solid walls. Suddenly, our isolated networks were linked to a global web, where the sheer scale of communication and data exchange outpaced the traditional security models. I recall the excitement—and the unease—that came with this change. At first, it seemed that a simple firewall could manage the few protocols that traversed the network boundary. The idea was straightforward: let the firewall be the gatekeeper, and if you were on the inside, you were trusted. The digital world was smaller then; protocols were fewer, and threats were less sophisticated. Yet, even then, subtle signs emerged that our trusted perimeter was beginning to show cracks.

Over time, these cracks widened. As businesses embraced digital transformation, we moved from a world of isolated systems to one of vast, interconnected networks where data flowed freely between on-premises systems and the emerging cloud. The explosion of mobile computing, remote work, and later the Internet of Things, fundamentally changed our relationship with technology. No longer could we rely on the idea that if you were inside the network, you were safe. I witnessed firsthand how attackers exploited the implicit trust that was extended to insiders and even remote workers. A single compromised credential could now lead to lateral movement across an entire organization. This was a wake-up call—a realization that our security models needed to evolve as rapidly as the technologies they were meant to protect.

Today, the landscape is unrecognizable compared to those early days. We have entered an era where the digital environment is vast, complex, and perpetually in motion. In our modern world, the traditional fortress with its high walls and guarded gates has given way to a dynamic, borderless realm. It is here that Zero Trust has emerged as a revolutionary approach. Zero Trust isn't just a set of technical controls; it is a philosophy that demands we assume nothing, verify everything, and continuously earn trust rather than granting it by default. I have seen the early seeds of this idea take root when cybersecurity experts began questioning the old adage that being inside the network automatically meant you were safe. They challenged the status quo, arguing that in a world of constant connectivity and sophisticated threats, the only reliable defense was to treat every user, every device, and every transaction as untrusted until proven otherwise.

Working through the decades, I have seen cybersecurity mature from a focus on physical security and simple network defenses to a complex discipline that blends technology, policy, and culture. I have watched as organizations struggled with breaches, learning painful lessons about the dangers of complacency and the pitfalls of over-reliance on traditional methods. With each incident, we learned more about how attackers operate—how they can bypass static defenses, exploit weak points, and move laterally once they gain a foothold. It became increasingly clear that our old models, which had served us well for a time, were no longer sufficient to protect the multifaceted, interconnected digital assets of today.

Now, we find ourselves at a crossroads. On one side, we have the legacy approaches of the past—a time when security meant locking the doors and trusting those inside. On the other side, we have a future that demands continuous vigilance, dynamic responses, and a holistic view of risk. Zero Trust is the answer to that future. It is a framework that evolves with the threats it is designed to counter. It doesn't rest on static defenses; it adapts, learns, and continuously improves. Every access request is treated as a potential threat until it is verified. Every piece of data is guarded by layers of dynamic controls, and every user must prove their legitimacy with every interaction. In my career, I have witnessed how this approach transforms security from a reactive, checklist-driven process into a proactive, adaptive, and resilient strategy that can withstand even the most sophisticated cyberattacks.

What excites me most about Zero Trust is its ability to integrate technology with a fundamental shift in mindset. It's not merely about installing new software or updating firewalls; it's about rethinking what it means to trust in a digital world. In our current environment, where threats are both constant and ever-changing, traditional methods of security are simply no longer viable. The elegance of Zero Trust lies in its simplicity: never assume, always verify. Yet, this simple principle has profound implications. It challenges us to continuously monitor and assess every interaction, to treat every access attempt as if it might be an intrusion, and to enforce strict controls at every layer of our digital architecture.

I have seen organizations transform under the Zero Trust model—companies that once suffered repeated breaches now stand resilient, their systems fortified by the very principle that changed their mindset. It is a journey that involves not just technology, but a complete cultural shift. In many of the organizations I've worked with over the years, security was once seen as a barrier—a necessary evil that slowed down business operations. Now, with Zero Trust, security is reimagined as an enabler. It allows businesses to innovate and expand without the looming fear of catastrophic breaches. By continuously verifying every interaction and dynamically adjusting to new threats, Zero Trust transforms security from a reactive posture into a proactive, strategic asset.

I have been fortunate enough to witness the evolution firsthand. I recall the early days when securing a network was as simple as ensuring that a physical lock was in place on a server room door. Today, securing a network is a sophisticated art —an interplay of advanced analytics, continuous monitoring, identity verification, and the relentless pursuit of improvement. I have seen technology evolve from rudimentary firewalls and antivirus programs to integrated systems that use artificial intelligence and machine learning to predict and counter threats in real time. I have observed how the security industry has shifted from reactive responses to breaches to a proactive strategy of prevention and rapid containment.

Looking ahead, I see a future where Zero Trust is not just a concept but a ubiquitous reality. Emerging technologies such as quantum computing and blockchain promise to further enhance our security capabilities, offering new tools to protect data in ways we could only imagine a few years ago. I envision a world where every digital interaction is continuously verified by systems so advanced that they can detect anomalies and preempt attacks before they occur. This is a future where security is seamlessly integrated into every facet of our digital lives—a future where the old days of implicit trust and static defenses are relegated to history.

As I reflect on the decades of evolution that have brought us to this point, I am filled with a sense of both nostalgia and excitement. I remember a time when the concept of cyber threats was almost foreign, when the security challenges were tangible and confined to physical locations. Today, we stand on the cusp of a new era—a world where the digital realm is as real and as critical as the physical one, and where our security strategies must evolve to meet the demands of a borderless, dynamic environment. The journey to Zero Trust is not just about technology; it is about a fundamental shift in how we perceive risk, trust, and responsibility in a world where every connection is an opportunity and every interaction must be earned.

This book is a culmination of my experiences, lessons learned, and the insights gathered over a lifetime in the field of cybersecurity. It is intended to serve as both a guide and a call to action for anyone who is serious about protecting their digital assets in an age where threats are constantly evolving. Whether you are a seasoned security professional, a business leader navigating the complexities of modern IT, or a curious mind seeking to understand the future of digital security, I hope that the principles and practices outlined in these pages will inspire you to think differently about trust and protection.

I invite you to join me on this journey—a journey that spans decades of evolution, from the isolated networks of the past to the complex, dynamic digital ecosystems of today. Let us embrace the challenge of never trusting by default, but always verifying, and in doing so, create a future where our digital world is not only secure but also resilient, agile, and ready to face the unknown challenges of tomorrow.

INTRODUCTION

The digital age has irrevocably transformed every facet of our lives, and among the most profound changes is how we protect the sensitive data and critical systems that underpin modern society. In a world that is increasingly interconnected and where the boundaries between internal networks and the public internet have all but disappeared, the traditional approach of building a strong, impenetrable wall around an organization's digital assets is no longer sufficient. The concept of Zero Trust emerges as a revolutionary framework in this environment —a philosophy that rejects the old notion of inherent trust simply because a user or device is inside the network. Instead, Zero Trust mandates that every access attempt must be continuously verified, regardless of its origin. This book, titled Zero Trust: Redefining Security in a Perimeterless World, is a comprehensive exploration of this transformative security paradigm and a roadmap for organizations seeking to navigate the ever-evolving landscape of cyber threats.

In the early days of computing, networks were isolated, and the conventional wisdom was simple: secure the perimeter, and you secure the data. The notion was that if you built a robust firewall around your network, the internal environment could be trusted implicitly. This approach, much like the fortified walls of a medieval castle, was effective when networks were small and contained within a physical space. However, as technology evolved and the digital landscape expanded to include remote work, cloud computing, mobile devices, and the Internet of Things, the very definition of a network perimeter began to blur. Today, employees can access corporate resources from coffee shops, home offices, or even while traveling abroad, and data flows freely between on-premises systems and a myriad of cloud services. In this interconnected reality, the traditional model of "if you're inside, you're safe" has proven to be dangerously outdated.

Zero Trust, by contrast, challenges that assumption at its very core. It operates on the principle that trust is not something granted by default; rather, it must be continuously earned and rigorously verified. Every request for access—whether it originates from an employee in a corporate office or from a remote worker using a personal device—is treated as if it comes from an untrusted source. This philosophy is best captured in the simple yet powerful adage: never trust, always verify. The implications of this shift are profound. By insisting on continuous authentication, real-time monitoring, and strict access controls, Zero Trust transforms how organizations approach cybersecurity, making it possible to limit damage even in the event of a breach and to adapt dynamically to emerging threats.

The evolution toward Zero Trust has not occurred in a vacuum. It is a response to a series of technological, operational, and cultural changes that have upended traditional security models. Over the past few decades, cyber attackers have grown more sophisticated, employing tactics that exploit the implicit trust of internal networks. Insider threats, once considered rare, are now recognized as one of the most insidious risks facing organizations. A single compromised account can provide attackers with a foothold, allowing them to move laterally across the network and access a vast array of sensitive information. These developments have underscored the limitations of perimeter-based security and have fueled the rise of a new security mindset—one that demands that every user, device, and process continuously prove its legitimacy.

At the heart of Zero Trust is a deep understanding of the complexities of trust in the digital age. Trust, as it has traditionally been understood in the realm of cybersecurity, was often a binary concept: either a user was trusted, or they were not. However, this simplistic view fails to capture the nuances of modern digital interactions. Credentials can be stolen or misused, devices can become compromised, and even trusted insiders can inadvertently create vulnerabilities. Zero Trust abandons the idea of inherent trust and instead embraces a dynamic, context-aware approach. Every access attempt is evaluated in real time against a multitude of factors such as user behavior, device integrity, location, and even time of day. This continuous process of verification not only helps to prevent unauthorized access but also limits the impact of any breach that might occur by ensuring that attackers are confined to the smallest possible segment of the network.

The journey toward Zero Trust is as much about technology as it is about a transformation in mindset and organizational culture. For many organizations, the shift represents a complete departure from the security practices that have been in place for decades. It is a journey from complacency to vigilance, from assuming trust to earning it with every interaction. This book will guide you through that journey by exploring the foundational concepts of Zero Trust, the technical architectures that make it possible, the cultural and operational changes required for successful implementation, and the future trends that will continue to shape this evolving security landscape.

One of the central tenets of Zero Trust is continuous verification. Rather than granting access based solely on an initial authentication event, every subsequent access attempt is subject to real-time evaluation. This means that even if a user has been authenticated in the past, they must constantly revalidate their identity and context. This approach is akin to an airport security system where, even after passing through the initial checkpoint, passengers may be subject to random additional screening throughout their journey. The goal is to ensure that the environment remains secure even if one layer of defense is compromised. In practice, this might involve multi-factor authentication, real-time behavioral analytics, and context-sensitive access controls that dynamically adjust based on the user's current situation. As we will see throughout this book, continuous verification is not just a technical requirement —it is a fundamental shift in how we conceive of trust in a digital world.

Another key principle of Zero Trust is the enforcement of the principle of least privilege. This concept dictates that every user and device should have only the minimum level of access required to perform their specific functions. By strictly limiting access, organizations can reduce the potential damage that might result from a compromised account or device. Imagine a scenario in which an employee is given broad access to all parts of a network versus one where the employee has access only to the specific resources needed for their role. In the latter case, even if that employee's credentials are stolen, the attacker's ability to cause harm is significantly curtailed. This principle is implemented through robust identity and access management systems, role-based access controls, and micro-segmentation techniques that create isolated compartments within the network. These strategies work together to ensure that even if a breach occurs in one area, the overall integrity of the system remains intact.

The concept of micro-segmentation is one of the most innovative aspects of Zero Trust. Traditional networks often functioned as a single, flat entity where, once inside, a user could move freely between different systems and data stores. Micro-segmentation challenges this notion by dividing the network into smaller, more secure segments, each governed by its own set of policies. This is similar to the design of a modern ship, where the hull is divided into compartments, and if one compartment is breached, the water is contained, preventing the entire ship from sinking. In a Zero Trust environment, even if an attacker gains access to one segment of the network, they are prevented from moving laterally to other segments. This not only limits the damage caused by a breach but also makes it much easier for security teams to detect and contain threats before they spread.

In addition to these technical strategies, the shift to Zero Trust represents a broader cultural and organizational transformation. For many companies, security has traditionally been seen as the sole responsibility of the IT department— a function that is separate from the day-to-day operations of the business. Zero Trust challenges this notion by embedding security into every layer of the organization. It requires that every employee, from senior executives to entry-level staff, understand that security is a shared responsibility. This cultural shift is critical because technology alone cannot protect against all threats; human behavior plays a crucial role in maintaining a secure environment. Training, awareness programs, and clear communication are essential components of this transformation. Employees must be educated not only on the technical aspects of security but also on the underlying philosophy of continuous verification and risk management. By fostering a culture where every action is seen as an opportunity to contribute to the overall security of the organization, companies can create a more resilient and proactive workforce.

The regulatory landscape also plays a significant role in shaping the evolution of Zero Trust. In recent years, governments and regulatory bodies around the world have enacted stringent data protection and privacy laws that require organizations to implement robust security measures. Regulations such as the European Union's General Data Protection Regulation (GDPR), the Health Insurance Portability and Accountability Act (HIPAA) in the United States, and the California Consumer Privacy Act (CCPA) impose strict requirements on how personal data is handled, stored, and secured. Zero Trust, with its emphasis on continuous monitoring, granular access controls, and detailed audit trails, is well suited to meet these regulatory challenges. By ensuring that every access request is verified and every interaction is logged, organizations can not only protect sensitive data but also demonstrate compliance with complex legal and regulatory requirements. This alignment between security practices and regulatory standards is essential for building trust with customers and partners in a world where data breaches can have far-reaching consequences.

Looking to the future, the evolution of Zero Trust will be driven by continuous technological innovation. Emerging technologies such as artificial intelligence, machine learning, quantum computing, and blockchain will further enhance the capabilities of Zero Trust frameworks. For example, as AI and machine learning algorithms become more sophisticated, they will be able to analyze vast amounts of data in real time, identifying subtle patterns and anomalies that may indicate a potential breach. This will allow for even more precise and proactive security measures, where threats can be detected and neutralized before they have a chance to cause significant harm. Quantum computing, while posing new challenges for encryption and data protection, will also spur the development of quantum-resistant algorithms that ensure data remains secure even against the most powerful computational threats. Blockchain technology, with its decentralized and immutable ledger, holds promise for revolutionizing identity management and access logging, providing a tamper-proof record of every transaction and access attempt. These innovations will not only strengthen the technical foundations of Zero Trust but will also create new opportunities for organizations to integrate security into every aspect of their operations.

The future of Zero Trust is also intertwined with the ongoing transformation of the modern workplace. The rise of remote work, accelerated by global events and changing work habits, has fundamentally altered the way organizations operate. In this new environment, employees access corporate resources from a multitude of locations using a diverse array of devices. This distributed nature of work requires a security model that is flexible, adaptive, and capable of continuously verifying every access request regardless of where it originates. Zero Trust provides the framework for this transformation by ensuring that security is maintained even when the traditional network perimeter no longer exists. As remote work continues to grow in prevalence, organizations that adopt Zero Trust will be better equipped to protect their data, maintain business continuity, and foster a culture of security across a distributed workforce.

The principles of Zero Trust are not static; they represent a mindset of continuous improvement and adaptation. In a world where cyber threats are constantly evolving, the only way to stay ahead is to embrace a security strategy that is as dynamic as the challenges it faces. Every breach, every near-miss, and every success is an opportunity to learn and improve. This iterative process is akin to the art of gardening, where a gardener must continuously tend to their plants—watering, pruning, and nurturing them to ensure a bountiful harvest. Similarly, organizations must cultivate their security posture through regular assessments, updates, and enhancements to ensure that they remain resilient in the face of new threats.

The journey to a Zero Trust world is a collective endeavor that requires unwavering commitment from every level of an organization. Leadership must set the tone by championing security initiatives and allocating the necessary resources to support the transformation. At the same time, every employee must understand that security is not an abstract concept reserved for the IT department, but a tangible, everyday practice that impacts the entire organization. Training, communication, and collaboration are essential in building a culture where continuous verification becomes second nature—a culture where every interaction is an opportunity to strengthen security and build trust.

As we look to the future, it is clear that the evolution of Zero Trust will continue to shape the landscape of cybersecurity for years to come. Emerging technologies, evolving threat landscapes, regulatory pressures, and cultural transformations will all play a role in driving this evolution. Organizations that embrace the principles of Zero Trust will not only protect their critical assets but will also position themselves for long-term success in an increasingly interconnected world. The promise of Zero Trust lies in its ability to transform security from a reactive, checklist-based process into a proactive, adaptive, and dynamic system—one that is capable of withstanding the challenges of today and tomorrow.

This book is an invitation to embark on that transformative journey. It is a call to reimagine how we think about security, to challenge the old paradigms, and to embrace a model where every access is verified, every risk is assessed, and every interaction contributes to a more secure digital environment. The chapters that follow will delve into the technical architectures, practical implementations, cultural shifts, and future trends that define Zero Trust. They will provide detailed case studies, real-world examples, and actionable insights to guide organizations on their path to adopting a Zero Trust framework. Whether you are a seasoned cybersecurity professional, a business leader looking to safeguard your organization's digital assets, or someone new to the world of cybersecurity, the principles and practices explored in these pages will equip you with the knowledge and tools needed to navigate the complex, ever-changing landscape of modern digital security.

As you read this book, consider it not as an endpoint, but as a starting point—a roadmap for continuous improvement and adaptation. The journey to Zero Trust is ongoing, and the lessons learned along the way will serve as a foundation for building a more resilient, agile, and trustworthy digital future. In a world where the only constant is change, the commitment to never trust by default, but always verify, will be the cornerstone of a secure and prosperous digital age.

In conclusion, the introduction to this book sets the stage for a deep dive into the world of Zero Trust—a security paradigm that redefines trust in a perimeterless world. It is a journey that challenges traditional notions of security and compels us to embrace a mindset of continuous verification and adaptive defense. The future of cybersecurity depends on our ability to rethink, innovate, and work together to build systems that are not only secure but also resilient in the face of an ever-changing threat landscape. As you embark on this journey, remember that every step, every challenge, and every success contributes to a collective mission: to create a digital future where trust is earned, risk is managed dynamically, and security is an enduring, integral part of our interconnected world.

CHAPTER 1: THE FOUNDATIONS OF ZERO TRUST

In the early days of digital networking, organizations believed that securing the boundaries of their systems was sufficient to protect their most sensitive information. The prevailing model of cybersecurity was simple and intuitive: build a strong wall around the enterprise's network, and once an adversary was kept out, the inner workings of the system could be trusted. This approach, often compared to the fortified walls of medieval castles, worked reasonably well in an era when networks were isolated and access was restricted to a small, trusted group of users. However, as technology evolved and connectivity expanded, the assumptions underpinning this model began to crumble. The interconnected nature of modern networks, spurred by the rise of the internet and mobile computing, rendered the traditional perimeter defense obsolete. It became increasingly clear that a breach of the outer defenses could allow an attacker to move freely within the network, accessing sensitive data and systems that were previously considered safe. This realization was the seed from which the concept of Zero Trust would eventually grow.

Over time, cyber attackers became more sophisticated, and the traditional defenses that had once provided a semblance of security started to show significant vulnerabilities. Incidents of insider threats, where trusted users intentionally or inadvertently caused harm, began to underscore a fundamental flaw in the old model: the assumption that internal network users were inherently trustworthy. The inadequacies of perimeter-based security were laid bare by breaches that exploited the implicit trust extended to anyone who had made it past the gate. This evolution in the threat landscape prompted a rethinking of security strategies among researchers and practitioners alike. Rather than assuming that the internal network was safe, the emerging paradigm proposed that every access request, regardless of its origin, should be treated with skepticism. Thus, the principle of "never trust, always verify" emerged as the cornerstone of a new security philosophy.

The origins of Zero Trust can be traced to a growing body of thought that questioned the validity of traditional trust models. Early research in the field of network security began to explore the idea that trust should not be granted based solely on network location. Instead, trust needed to be earned through continuous authentication, rigorous verification of identity, and the enforcement of strict access controls. This paradigm shift was not merely a reaction to the increasing sophistication of cyber threats; it was also an acknowledgement that the nature of modern work had changed. With the proliferation of remote work, cloud computing, and the Internet of Things, the very notion of a defined network perimeter had become meaningless. Devices and users now operated in a dispersed, dynamic environment where the boundaries between the corporate network and the public internet were blurred, if not entirely erased.

At the heart of Zero Trust is a profound understanding of the complexities and nuances of trust in the digital age. Traditional security models operated on the assumption that once a user or device was authenticated, it could be trusted to behave appropriately. However, this approach failed to account for the reality that credentials could be compromised, devices could be infected with malware, and insider threats could originate from within the organization. Zero Trust rejects the binary notion of trust and instead embraces a more granular approach, where trust is continuously evaluated and recalibrated based on a variety of factors, including user behavior, device health, location, and contextual risk. This continuous process of evaluation ensures that even if a breach occurs, the attacker's ability to move laterally within the network is severely restricted.

The evolution of cybersecurity into a Zero Trust model is also a story of technological progress and the challenges of managing complex systems. In the not-so-distant past, network infrastructures were relatively simple, and the number of users and devices was manageable. With the exponential growth of data and the advent of sophisticated applications, the modern enterprise now encompasses an intricate web of interconnected systems that span on-premises data centers, cloud environments, and remote endpoints. This complexity creates a fertile ground for security vulnerabilities, as traditional models were ill-equipped to handle the dynamic nature of modern IT ecosystems. The need for a more adaptive, resilient approach to security became increasingly apparent, setting the stage for the development of Zero Trust principles.

In embracing Zero Trust, organizations are compelled to rethink not only their technical architectures but also their organizational cultures and processes. The shift towards a Zero Trust environment is as much about transforming the mindset of security professionals as it is about implementing new technologies. It requires a commitment to continuous improvement and a willingness to challenge long-held assumptions about what constitutes a secure environment. This transformation often begins with a thorough understanding of the current state of security within the organization, including a careful analysis of where vulnerabilities exist and how data flows between different parts of the network. By mapping out these pathways, security professionals can begin to design a system where every access request is scrutinized, and no user or device is automatically granted unfettered access simply because it resides behind the corporate firewall.

The core tenets of Zero Trust—continuous verification, least privilege access, and micro-segmentation—are not new ideas in themselves, but their combined application represents a significant departure from traditional security practices.

Continuous verification means that every request for access is treated as if it originates from an untrusted source, regardless of whether the request comes from inside or outside the organization's network. This approach requires robust mechanisms for authenticating users and devices at every step of the process. In many ways, it is a natural extension of the multi-factor authentication techniques that have become commonplace in recent years. However, Zero Trust takes this concept further by insisting on ongoing validation rather than a one-time check at the point of entry.

Least privilege access is another fundamental principle that underpins the Zero Trust model. The idea is simple: users and devices should be granted only the minimum level of access necessary to perform their functions. This principle is a direct response to the vulnerabilities exposed by overly permissive access policies, where a single compromised account could lead to a cascade of security failures. By limiting access rights and ensuring that each user's permissions are tightly controlled, organizations can significantly reduce the potential impact of a breach. The implementation of least privilege is often supported by sophisticated role-based access control systems that dynamically adjust permissions based on the context of the request. Over time, this approach has proven to be a powerful tool in mitigating the risks associated with insider threats and credential theft.

Micro-segmentation is a more recent innovation that has gained traction in the era of Zero Trust. It involves dividing the network into smaller, isolated segments, each with its own set of security policies. By compartmentalizing the network, organizations can contain breaches more effectively, preventing an attacker from moving laterally once they have gained access to a single segment. This strategy is akin to compartmentalizing a ship to prevent it from sinking when a single compartment is breached. In practice, micro-segmentation requires a detailed understanding of the network's topology and the interactions between different components. It often leverages software-defined networking technologies to create dynamic, policy-driven segments that can adapt to changing threat conditions.

The journey toward Zero Trust is not without its challenges. One of the primary obstacles is the inherent tension between usability and security. Traditional security models often prioritize ease of access and convenience, sometimes at the expense of rigorous security measures. Implementing Zero Trust requires organizations to adopt a more disciplined approach to access management, which can sometimes be perceived as burdensome by end users. However, the long-term benefits of a Zero Trust model—in terms of both enhanced security and the ability to adapt to emerging threats—far outweigh the initial inconvenience. As organizations become more familiar with the principles of Zero Trust, they typically find that the approach not only improves security posture but also fosters a more proactive, resilient culture.

A significant aspect of adopting Zero Trust involves understanding and defining the terminology that underpins the model. The language of Zero Trust is replete with terms that may seem technical or even arcane to those unfamiliar with modern cybersecurity. Concepts such as lateral movement, continuous monitoring, identity federation, and context-aware security have become integral to the discourse around Zero Trust. While these terms can be daunting at first, they represent essential building blocks for constructing a robust security framework. For instance, lateral movement refers to the techniques used by attackers to move across a network once they have gained initial access. In a Zero Trust environment, strategies are implemented to detect and block lateral movement, thereby containing potential breaches. Similarly, continuous monitoring ensures that every interaction within the network is scrutinized for signs of anomalous behavior. By establishing a common vocabulary, organizations can better align their security practices with the evolving demands of the digital landscape.

The evolution of Zero Trust has been driven not only by technological advances but also by a series of high-profile security breaches that have reshaped public and corporate attitudes toward cybersecurity. Major incidents involving the theft of sensitive data and the disruption of critical services have served as wake-up calls for organizations across the globe. These events have underscored the limitations of traditional security models and accelerated the adoption of Zero Trust strategies. In many cases, the transition to a Zero Trust model has been catalyzed by the realization that the old paradigms simply could not keep pace with the speed and sophistication of modern cyber threats. The fallout from these breaches has often led to a reevaluation of security policies, prompting organizations to invest in new technologies and strategies that emphasize continuous verification and adaptive security controls.

As the concept of Zero Trust gained traction, it also began to influence the broader discourse on cybersecurity. Thought leaders and industry experts started to advocate for a fundamental rethinking of how trust is established in digital environments. Rather than viewing trust as a static, binary state, they proposed that trust should be viewed as a dynamic continuum, subject to ongoing assessment and adjustment. This shift in perspective has profound implications for how security is managed at every level of an organization. It calls for a holistic approach that integrates technology, processes, and human factors into a cohesive framework. The realization that trust must be earned rather than assumed has led to the development of innovative security architectures that are more resilient, flexible, and capable of withstanding the myriad threats of the modern world.

In many respects, the adoption of Zero Trust represents a philosophical shift as much as it does a technical one. It challenges the long-held belief that security can be achieved through rigid controls and static defenses. Instead, Zero Trust posits that security is an ongoing process, one that requires constant vigilance, adaptability, and a willingness to challenge established norms. This perspective has profound implications for the way organizations approach risk management. It encourages a culture of continuous improvement, where security measures are regularly reassessed and refined in response to new threats and vulnerabilities. Over time, this proactive stance has proven to be essential in maintaining a robust defense against an ever-evolving landscape of cyber threats.

The transition to a Zero Trust model is not an overnight transformation but rather a gradual process of evolution. Organizations must first come to terms with the limitations of their existing security frameworks and be willing to invest in the technologies and processes that enable continuous verification and adaptive access controls. This journey often begins with a comprehensive assessment of current systems and practices, followed by the identification of critical vulnerabilities and the development of a roadmap for change. Throughout this process, it is imperative that all stakeholders, from top-level executives to frontline employees, are brought into the conversation. The success of a Zero Trust implementation depends on a collective commitment to rethinking how trust is established and maintained in the digital environment.

As organizations embark on this journey, they are likely to encounter a range of challenges. The cultural shift required to embrace a Zero Trust mindset can be as daunting as the technical challenges involved in overhauling existing systems. Resistance to change is a natural human tendency, and many organizations struggle to move away from established practices that have been in place for decades. Overcoming this inertia requires not only a clear articulation of the benefits of Zero Trust but also a willingness to invest in education and training. By fostering an environment where security is viewed as a shared responsibility, organizations can help ensure that all members of the workforce understand the critical importance of continuous verification and adaptive security measures.

Despite these challenges, the benefits of adopting a Zero Trust model are substantial. In an era where cyber threats are becoming increasingly sophisticated and pervasive, the ability to dynamically assess and mitigate risk is invaluable. Zero Trust offers a pathway to a more secure, resilient, and adaptable cybersecurity posture, one that is capable of withstanding the complexities of the modern digital landscape. By shifting the focus from static defenses to dynamic, context-aware security controls, organizations can significantly reduce the risk of catastrophic breaches and ensure that sensitive data remains protected even in the face of determined adversaries.

The foundational principles of Zero Trust—continuous verification, least privilege, and micro-segmentation—serve as guiding lights for organizations seeking to navigate the turbulent waters of modern cybersecurity. Each principle reinforces the others, creating a cohesive framework that is greater than the sum of its parts. Continuous verification ensures that every access request is scrutinized, while least privilege limits the potential damage of any single breach by restricting access to only what is absolutely necessary. Micro-segmentation further isolates potential threats, preventing them from spreading unchecked across the network. Together, these principles form the bedrock of a security model that is both robust and adaptable, capable of responding to emerging threats in real time.

The journey toward Zero Trust is one marked by both innovation and adaptation. It represents a departure from the complacency of old models and an embrace of a more dynamic, proactive approach to cybersecurity. As organizations continue to grapple with the challenges of a hyper-connected world, the principles of Zero Trust will undoubtedly play an increasingly critical role in shaping the future of digital security. The evolution of this model is a testament to the fact that in the realm of cybersecurity, there are no permanent solutions—only ongoing processes of assessment, adaptation, and improvement. In this context, the foundations of Zero Trust are not just a set of technical guidelines but a philosophical commitment to the idea that security must be as fluid and adaptable as the threats it seeks to counter.

Looking back at the early days of network security, one can see how the lessons learned from decades of defending against cyber threats have converged into a coherent strategy that emphasizes vigilance, adaptability, and a refusal to take anything for granted. The shift from a perimeter-based model to one that treats every access request as potentially untrustworthy is emblematic of a broader trend in cybersecurity —a recognition that the traditional notions of safety and trust are no longer adequate in the face of modern challenges. The foundations of Zero Trust are built on the understanding that security must evolve continuously, that it must anticipate and adapt to threats rather than simply react to them. This proactive approach is what sets Zero Trust apart from its predecessors, offering a roadmap for a future where security is embedded in every interaction, every transaction, and every connection.

As the digital landscape continues to change at a breakneck pace, the principles of Zero Trust offer a guiding framework for organizations seeking to protect their assets in an increasingly complex world. The emphasis on continuous verification, the rigorous enforcement of least privilege, and the strategic use of micro-segmentation are all reflections of a broader understanding: that in today's world, trust must be earned, not assumed. This realization has profound implications for how organizations structure their security policies and invest in technology. It demands a level of discipline and attention to detail that goes beyond the traditional checklists of firewalls and antivirus software. Instead, it requires a holistic approach, one that integrates advanced analytics, real-time monitoring, and a deep understanding of user behavior into every aspect of the security infrastructure.

The story of Zero Trust is ultimately a story of transformation —a journey from complacency to vigilance, from assumption to verification. It is a journey that challenges long-held beliefs about the nature of security and calls for a reevaluation of how trust is established in the digital age. For those who undertake this journey, the rewards can be substantial. A robust Zero Trust framework not only mitigates the risks of cyber attacks but also empowers organizations to operate with greater confidence in an environment where threats are constantly evolving. It provides a clear, actionable path forward in a landscape that is often characterized by uncertainty and rapid change.

In reflecting on the evolution of cybersecurity and the emergence of Zero Trust, one is reminded of the timeless adage that "the only constant is change." The digital world is in a perpetual state of flux, and the strategies that once served as effective safeguards can quickly become outdated in the face of new challenges. Zero Trust embodies this understanding by advocating for a model of security that is as dynamic and adaptable as the threats it seeks to counter. It is a model built not on static defenses, but on a continuous process of learning, adaptation, and improvement—a process that recognizes that in the battle against cyber threats, complacency is the enemy.

The foundation of Zero Trust is, therefore, more than just a set of technical measures or security protocols; it is a comprehensive approach to risk management that permeates every level of an organization. It requires a deep commitment to rethinking established practices, to challenging assumptions about what constitutes trust and safety in the digital realm. It is an approach that calls for collaboration across disciplines and a willingness to embrace new technologies and methodologies in the pursuit of a more secure future. In this light, the journey toward Zero Trust is not merely a technical upgrade but a fundamental shift in perspective—a recognition that the security challenges of the modern era demand a new way of thinking about trust, risk, and protection.

As organizations continue to navigate the complexities of a hyper-connected world, the principles that form the foundation of Zero Trust will serve as an enduring guide. They remind us that in the face of relentless cyber threats, the only effective strategy is one that is built on constant vigilance, continuous improvement, and an unwavering commitment to verifying every interaction. The evolution of Zero Trust is a powerful testament to the transformative potential of this approach—a potential that promises to redefine the landscape of cybersecurity for years to come. In embracing this philosophy, organizations not only enhance their defenses but also lay the groundwork for a more resilient and adaptable future, one in which trust is not given lightly but earned through a relentless pursuit of security excellence.

Ultimately, the story of Zero Trust is a story about the evolution of security in a world where the stakes have never been higher. It is a narrative of adaptation, innovation, and the relentless pursuit of a more secure and resilient digital ecosystem. As we look to the future, it is clear that the principles of Zero Trust will continue to shape the strategies and technologies that underpin our collective efforts to safeguard information in an ever-changing threat landscape. The journey may be challenging, but the rewards—a more secure, dynamic, and trusted digital world —are well worth the effort.

CHAPTER 2: ZERO TRUST ARCHITECTURE

In a world where traditional network boundaries have all but dissolved, the architecture that underpins modern cybersecurity must be as agile and adaptable as the threats it faces. The concept of Zero Trust Architecture emerged as a response to the limitations of perimeter-based defenses and has since evolved into a comprehensive framework that redefines how organizations secure their networks, data, and users. This new architecture is not merely a collection of tools or a checklist of best practices; it is a fundamental shift in how we perceive trust, network design, and risk management.

The journey into Zero Trust Architecture begins with the recognition that the era of clearly defined network perimeters is over. Once, the security model was built around a strong external defense—a firewall that separated the trusted internal environment from the chaotic external world. However, as organizations embraced digital transformation, mobile computing, cloud services, and the proliferation of Internet of Things devices, the traditional boundaries blurred. In this landscape, the notion of a "trusted" zone shrank to nearly nothing, and the inherent trust that was once extended simply by virtue of being inside the network was no longer a viable assumption. Instead, every access request, whether coming from a corporate office, a remote home office, or a mobile device in a coffee shop, must be treated with the same level of scrutiny.

At the heart of Zero Trust Architecture lies the principle of continuous verification. Rather than relying on a one-time check at the point of entry, every interaction is treated as a potential risk that requires constant authentication and authorization. In practice, this means that every device, user, or application attempting to access a resource is continuously evaluated against a set of dynamically changing policies. These policies are informed by factors such as user identity, device health, location, and real-time threat intelligence. The architecture is designed to be adaptive, constantly assessing the context of a request, and only granting access on a strictly need-to-know basis. This continuous validation creates a dynamic security posture that evolves in response to emerging risks and changing operational conditions.

One of the most significant innovations within Zero Trust Architecture is the concept of micro-segmentation. Traditional networks often operated with a "flat" architecture where, once inside, users had broad access to many resources. In contrast, micro-segmentation divides the network into isolated zones, each governed by its own strict policies. By breaking the network into smaller segments, any breach or compromise in one segment does not automatically provide an attacker unfettered access to the entire network. The segmentation is enforced through software-defined controls that adapt to traffic patterns and user behavior, ensuring that even if an attacker were to infiltrate one segment, lateral movement would be severely restricted. This granular control over data flows and communications creates multiple layers of defense, each one reinforcing the overall security of the system.

The role of identity and access management (IAM) in a Zero Trust Architecture cannot be overstated. In a traditional security model, authentication was often a one-time event, but in a Zero Trust environment, identity verification is an ongoing process. Multi-factor authentication is standard, and it is complemented by continuous behavioral monitoring that detects anomalies in how a user interacts with the system. If a normally cautious employee suddenly starts accessing sensitive data at odd hours, the system raises an alert or even automatically revokes access pending further verification. The idea is to treat every access attempt as a potential security incident, ensuring that no single credential—no matter how seemingly secure—becomes the Achilles' heel of the organization.

Another critical element of Zero Trust Architecture is the integration of endpoint security into the broader network defense strategy. In the past, devices were often considered secure once they were inside the corporate network. Today, endpoints such as laptops, smartphones, and IoT devices are viewed as independent entities that require constant monitoring and management. Each device is assessed for its security posture, including its operating system, patch level, and any signs of compromise. This information feeds into the larger Zero Trust framework, influencing access decisions in real time. A device that suddenly shows signs of vulnerability might be isolated from critical resources until it can be remediated. By integrating endpoint security into the overall architecture, organizations create a more resilient environment where every potential point of entry is scrutinized and secured.

Cloud integration presents both challenges and opportunities within Zero Trust Architecture. As organizations migrate critical applications and data to the cloud, the traditional concept of a centralized, on-premises network becomes obsolete. Instead, cloud resources are distributed across multiple platforms and locations, each with its own security considerations. Zero Trust Architecture embraces this reality by extending its principles into the cloud, treating every cloud resource as if it were as vulnerable as an on-premises server. This approach requires close coordination between cloud providers and internal security systems, with policies that are enforced consistently across all environments. The ability to maintain a unified security posture, regardless of where data or applications reside, is a hallmark of a mature Zero Trust implementation.

The dynamic nature of modern IT environments necessitates a security architecture that can adapt quickly to changes. Traditional models often relied on static rules and fixed defenses, but the Zero Trust approach is inherently agile. It leverages automation and real-time analytics to adjust access controls and security policies on the fly. For instance, if a sudden surge in suspicious activity is detected, the system can automatically tighten access controls, restrict certain actions, or trigger an alert for human intervention. This level of automation is essential in today's threat landscape, where attacks can escalate rapidly and require immediate responses. The ability to dynamically respond to emerging threats is one of the key advantages of Zero Trust Architecture, ensuring that security measures are always one step ahead of potential adversaries.

Zero Trust Architecture also redefines the relationship between network infrastructure and application design. In the past, applications were often developed with the assumption that they would operate in a secure, isolated environment. Today, applications must be designed to function securely even in a highly distributed and potentially hostile environment. This means incorporating security directly into the software development lifecycle, where every component of an application is designed with the expectation that it will be subject to continuous scrutiny. Developers work closely with security teams to implement robust access controls, encryption, and monitoring mechanisms that align with Zero Trust principles. This integrated approach not only enhances the security of the application but also makes it more resilient to attacks that target vulnerabilities in the code.

The transformation brought about by Zero Trust Architecture is not solely a technical challenge; it also represents a profound shift in organizational culture. Moving away from a model that assumes inherent trust within the network requires a reeducation of employees, stakeholders, and decision-makers. It demands a culture where security is seen as a shared responsibility, and where continuous improvement is not just encouraged but required. Organizations must invest in training and awareness programs to ensure that everyone understands the new paradigm and the role they play in maintaining a secure environment. This cultural shift is often one of the most challenging aspects of implementing Zero Trust, as it requires overcoming long-standing assumptions and practices that have been ingrained over decades.

One of the most transformative aspects of Zero Trust Architecture is its ability to integrate with emerging technologies that further enhance security. Artificial intelligence and machine learning, for example, play an increasingly important role in analyzing vast amounts of data in real time. These technologies enable the system to detect subtle patterns and anomalies that might indicate a security breach, often before human analysts would notice. By incorporating AI-driven analytics into the Zero Trust framework, organizations can achieve a level of proactive defense that anticipates and neutralizes threats more effectively. This integration not only improves the accuracy of threat detection but also reduces the workload on security teams, allowing them to focus on more strategic tasks.

The evolution of network architecture toward a Zero Trust model also raises important considerations about scalability and future-proofing. As organizations grow and their networks become more complex, the ability to maintain a consistent security posture becomes increasingly challenging. Zero Trust Architecture addresses this challenge by providing a modular, scalable framework that can be adapted to organizations of any size. Whether a company is a small startup or a multinational corporation, the principles of continuous verification, micro-segmentation, and dynamic access control remain applicable. This scalability ensures that as the organization expands, its security architecture can evolve in tandem, maintaining robust protection without imposing undue burdens on IT resources.

The implementation of Zero Trust Architecture is a journey marked by continuous learning and adaptation. Organizations often begin by assessing their current security posture and identifying areas where traditional models have fallen short. This initial assessment is critical, as it provides the foundation upon which a Zero Trust framework can be built. From there, the process involves designing new policies, integrating advanced technologies, and restructuring network layouts to support the granular controls that Zero Trust demands. This transition is rarely instantaneous; it is a gradual evolution that requires sustained effort, investment, and a willingness to challenge conventional wisdom. Yet, as organizations progress along this path, the benefits become increasingly apparent—a more resilient, adaptable, and secure network that can withstand the evolving threats of the digital age.

The shift to a Zero Trust Architecture also redefines the role of network monitoring and analytics. In a traditional setup, monitoring might have been limited to a few key points along the perimeter. However, in a Zero Trust environment, monitoring becomes ubiquitous and continuous. Every access request, data flow, and user interaction is logged and analyzed for signs of suspicious activity. This comprehensive approach to monitoring creates a rich dataset that can be mined for insights, allowing security teams to identify trends and potential vulnerabilities before they escalate into full-blown incidents. The use of advanced analytics, powered by both historical data and real-time inputs, transforms raw information into actionable intelligence. In this way, Zero Trust Architecture turns every network interaction into an opportunity to learn, adapt, and improve overall security.

The design of a Zero Trust network is inherently iterative. As new technologies emerge and threats evolve, the architecture must be continually refined and updated. This iterative process is facilitated by the modular nature of the framework, which allows organizations to add or replace components as needed without overhauling the entire system. For example, as new endpoint security solutions become available, they can be integrated into the existing architecture to provide enhanced protection. Similarly, as cloud providers roll out new security features, these can be incorporated seamlessly into the Zero Trust framework. This adaptability ensures that the architecture remains current and effective, even as the technological landscape shifts and evolves.

Beyond the technical components, Zero Trust Architecture also demands a reevaluation of traditional security policies and procedures. The shift away from inherent trust means that policies must be redefined to reflect a more granular, risk-based approach. Access controls, for instance, are no longer static and based solely on predefined roles; they must be dynamic, adapting to the context of each request. This often involves implementing sophisticated policy engines that can analyze a wide range of variables—from user behavior and device health to environmental factors such as time and location—and make real-time decisions about whether to grant access. The resulting policies are far more nuanced than their traditional counterparts, enabling organizations to strike a delicate balance between security and operational efficiency.

The integration of Zero Trust Architecture into existing IT environments can present significant challenges, particularly for organizations with legacy systems. Older systems may not have been designed with the level of granularity or flexibility required by Zero Trust principles, and retrofitting them can be a complex, resource-intensive process. Nonetheless, many organizations have found that the long-term benefits of a Zero Trust approach—such as reduced risk of lateral movement by attackers and improved incident response capabilities—justify the initial challenges of integration. In some cases, this may mean deploying intermediary technologies or building custom solutions to bridge the gap between legacy systems and modern security requirements. The end goal is a coherent, unified security posture that spans all parts of the organization, regardless of their age or technological sophistication.

As the conversation around cybersecurity increasingly

embraces Zero Trust, the architecture is also influencing the design of future networks. Many technology vendors and service providers are now building their solutions from the ground up with Zero Trust principles in mind. These next-generation products are designed to integrate seamlessly into a Zero Trust framework, offering built-in capabilities for continuous verification, adaptive access control, and real-time analytics. The result is a rapidly expanding ecosystem of tools and technologies that collectively enhance the security posture of organizations adopting Zero Trust. This trend is reshaping the market and setting new standards for what is expected in modern cybersecurity solutions.

Zero Trust Architecture is not a destination but an ongoing process—a journey that requires constant vigilance, continuous improvement, and the willingness to challenge the status quo. It demands an organizational mindset that views security as an evolving discipline, one where every component, process, and user must earn trust continuously. The architecture serves as both a technical framework and a strategic philosophy, guiding organizations as they navigate the complex and ever-changing landscape of digital threats. With its emphasis on continuous verification, granular control, and adaptive defense, Zero Trust Architecture offers a compelling vision for a future in which security is not an afterthought but a fundamental aspect of every interaction.

In reflecting on the development of Zero Trust Architecture, it is clear that this approach represents more than a set of technical innovations—it embodies a radical rethinking of how we conceptualize and implement security in the digital age. It challenges us to abandon the outdated models of yesterday and embrace a framework that is as fluid and dynamic as the networks it is designed to protect. As organizations continue to expand their digital footprints and adopt new technologies at an unprecedented pace, the principles of Zero Trust will undoubtedly remain at the forefront of cybersecurity strategy.

The architecture provides a resilient foundation upon which organizations can build robust defenses against an array of threats, ensuring that even in the most complex and distributed environments, security remains an ever-present priority.

Ultimately, Zero Trust Architecture is a testament to the evolving nature of cybersecurity—a discipline that must continuously adapt to the changing dynamics of technology and threat. It is an architecture that not only addresses the technical challenges of today but also anticipates the risks of tomorrow. In this way, it offers organizations a roadmap for building networks that are secure, agile, and capable of withstanding the relentless onslaught of cyber threats. As we move further into the era of digital transformation, the lessons learned from the implementation of Zero Trust Architecture will serve as a guiding light, illuminating the path toward a more secure and resilient future for all.

CHAPTER 3: PLANNING AND STRATEGY FOR ZERO TRUST ADOPTION

Embarking on the journey to adopt Zero Trust is not a simple task of installing new software or flipping a switch; it is an intricate transformation that touches every facet of an organization's operations, culture, and technology. In the early stages of this journey, leaders and security teams must step back to assess the existing landscape, recognize inherent vulnerabilities, and understand that the road ahead is not paved with quick fixes but with careful planning and strategic execution. The process begins with a deep, honest evaluation of the current security posture. This involves mapping the intricate network of systems, data flows, and user interactions that have been built up over years, if not decades, of operating under a traditional, perimeter-based model. Organizations need to develop a comprehensive inventory of their assets, identifying which systems hold sensitive data and which processes are most critical to business operations. This assessment often reveals hidden vulnerabilities, especially where legacy systems and outdated security practices have created blind spots in the defense posture.

Once the landscape is clearly understood, the next step is to conduct a rigorous risk assessment. This assessment is not limited to identifying which assets are vulnerable, but also extends to understanding the potential impact of a breach. It involves analyzing both internal and external threats and determining how these threats could exploit current weaknesses. Risk assessment in a Zero Trust context requires the organization to move beyond static evaluations and adopt a dynamic view of risk that continuously incorporates new intelligence and changing circumstances. The idea is to shift from a mindset of "if we build a big wall, we are safe" to one of constant vigilance where every interaction, whether from an internal employee or an external partner, is scrutinized based on the risk it might pose. This shift in thinking is both a technical and a cultural challenge, as it requires decision-makers to acknowledge that the traditional concept of a trusted internal network is no longer tenable.

The transformation to a Zero Trust framework begins with building a detailed roadmap that outlines short-term wins and long-term strategic goals. This roadmap is a living document that details the phased approach the organization will take to integrate Zero Trust principles into its infrastructure. At the outset, it is crucial to set realistic expectations. Organizations need to identify which areas can yield immediate improvements in security posture with relatively low investment and which parts of the network require more substantial overhauls. This phased approach might start with pilot projects in isolated segments of the network, allowing the team to test the new protocols, measure their effectiveness, and gradually expand successful initiatives across the enterprise. The roadmap also has to incorporate contingency plans and clearly defined milestones so that progress can be measured over time. It is not enough to simply have a plan on paper; the roadmap must be actionable, with each phase building upon the lessons learned from previous efforts and adjusting to emerging threats.

Integral to the planning process is the need for stakeholder engagement and organizational alignment. Zero Trust adoption is not solely the responsibility of the IT or security department; it requires buy-in from all levels of the organization. Senior executives must understand that this transformation is not just about technology, but about shifting the very culture of the organization towards one where security is embedded in every process and decision. This cultural change is challenging because it forces long-standing habits and assumptions to be reexamined. Leaders must communicate clearly and frequently about the importance of the change, illustrating both the potential benefits and the risks of inaction. They need to foster a sense of shared responsibility among all employees, ensuring that every individual understands their role in maintaining a secure environment. Training sessions, regular updates, and collaborative workshops become essential tools in this endeavor, as they help demystify the complexities of Zero Trust and encourage a proactive approach to security.

The financial implications of transitioning to a Zero Trust model also need to be carefully considered. Cost-benefit analysis plays a critical role in securing the necessary budget and resources for the project. On one hand, organizations must invest in new technologies, such as advanced identity and access management systems, endpoint security solutions, and network segmentation tools. On the other hand, they need to weigh these investments against the potential costs of a security breach —costs that include not only direct financial losses but also reputational damage and regulatory penalties. In many cases, a thorough cost-benefit analysis reveals that the long-term savings and risk mitigation provided by a Zero Trust strategy far outweigh the initial outlays. Such analyses are particularly important when justifying the project to stakeholders who may be more accustomed to traditional, perimeter-based security models. A compelling financial case can turn skepticism into support, especially when concrete data and case studies from similar organizations are presented.

As part of the planning process, it is essential to map out the integration of Zero Trust principles with existing legacy systems. Many organizations have invested heavily in systems that were built around the notion of a secure, static network environment. Transitioning these systems into a Zero Trust framework can be complex, as they may not have been designed to operate under continuous authentication and dynamic access controls. This integration challenge often requires creative solutions, such as deploying intermediary technologies or creating custom interfaces that allow legacy systems to communicate with modern security tools. In some instances, it may even necessitate a phased replacement of older systems with newer, more agile technologies. The goal is to ensure that the entire IT ecosystem, regardless of its age or original design, is brought into alignment with the Zero Trust philosophy. This process demands meticulous planning and a willingness to invest in incremental upgrades that, over time, result in a cohesive and resilient security architecture.

Beyond technical integration, the planning phase must address the human element of the transformation. People are often the weakest link in security, and the shift to Zero Trust is as much about altering behaviors and practices as it is about implementing new technologies. In a Zero Trust environment, every user must be treated as a potential risk until their identity and context are verified. This means rethinking access privileges and ensuring that employees are not granted more access than is absolutely necessary for their roles. Implementing the principle of least privilege involves not only technological adjustments but also a reassessment of job functions and responsibilities. Training programs become indispensable, as they equip employees with the knowledge to navigate a new security landscape where continuous verification and behavioral monitoring are the norm. In turn, these educational initiatives help cultivate an environment of accountability and shared vigilance, making it easier to spot and address deviations from expected behavior before they escalate into security incidents.

A comprehensive strategy for Zero Trust adoption must also incorporate robust metrics and key performance indicators (KPIs) that allow organizations to measure the success of their initiatives. These metrics go beyond traditional measures of security incidents or compliance audits; they encompass indicators such as the speed and accuracy of threat detection, the responsiveness of the system to emerging risks, and the overall reduction in lateral movement within the network. By establishing clear benchmarks and regularly reviewing performance data, organizations can continuously refine their security posture and ensure that the Zero Trust model is delivering on its promises. This feedback loop is essential not only for internal improvement but also for demonstrating the value of the transformation to external stakeholders, including customers, partners, and regulators. In many cases, improved metrics serve as a powerful testament to the effectiveness of the Zero Trust approach, reinforcing the decision to invest in this long-term strategy.

Implementing Zero Trust also requires the development of new policies and procedures that reflect the dynamic, risk-based nature of the model. Traditional security policies, which often relied on static roles and predefined access levels, must be reworked to incorporate continuous monitoring and adaptive access controls. This involves drafting policies that outline how and when access should be granted, detailing the circumstances under which privileges are elevated or revoked, and defining the protocols for handling potential security incidents. Policy development in a Zero Trust framework is a collaborative effort that involves input from various departments, including IT, legal, compliance, and human resources. The resulting policies are typically more nuanced and flexible, allowing the organization to respond quickly to changing conditions while maintaining a rigorous security posture. Over time, these policies are refined through iterative testing and feedback, ensuring that they remain effective in the face of evolving threats.

As part of the strategic planning, it is also critical to develop a robust incident response and recovery plan that aligns with Zero Trust principles. The assumption underlying Zero Trust is that breaches are not a matter of if, but when. Therefore, organizations must be prepared to respond swiftly and effectively to any security incident. This preparation involves creating detailed playbooks that specify the roles and responsibilities of each team member in the event of a breach, outlining the steps to isolate affected segments of the network, and establishing communication protocols to inform stakeholders and mitigate reputational damage. An effective incident response plan under a Zero Trust model leverages the granular visibility provided by continuous monitoring, enabling security teams to pinpoint the source of an incident quickly and limit its impact. In many cases, the ability to respond in a coordinated and efficient manner is what ultimately determines the severity of the breach's consequences. Therefore, incident response planning is not an afterthought but a core component of the overall Zero Trust strategy.

Throughout the planning process, leadership must recognize that adopting Zero Trust is not a one-time project but an ongoing commitment to security excellence. The dynamic nature of modern cyber threats means that the strategies and technologies implemented today may need to be revisited and updated tomorrow. This understanding should be embedded in the strategic vision from the very beginning. Organizations need to establish governance structures that ensure continuous review and adaptation of their security practices. Regular audits, both internal and external, become critical in validating that the Zero Trust framework is functioning as intended and identifying areas where improvements can be made. In this way, the strategy for Zero Trust adoption is itself a living, evolving blueprint that grows and adapts in tandem with the organization and its external environment.

As the planning phase matures, it becomes apparent that the path to Zero Trust is marked by a series of iterative cycles rather than a single transformative leap. Each phase of implementation provides valuable lessons that inform subsequent phases. Early successes, often achieved through pilot projects or targeted initiatives, build momentum and generate confidence among stakeholders. These early wins serve as a proof of concept, demonstrating that the principles of Zero Trust can indeed be translated into practical, effective security measures. At the same time, the challenges encountered during these initial phases—whether they relate to technology integration, policy development, or cultural resistance—offer critical insights into how the broader organization can better prepare for the full-scale adoption of the model. In this iterative process, flexibility is key. Leaders must be willing to adjust the roadmap as needed, embracing a mindset of continuous improvement that is essential for staying ahead of an ever-evolving threat landscape.

One of the most significant challenges during the planning and strategy phase is reconciling the need for rigorous security with the demands of operational efficiency. Organizations naturally strive to maintain smooth, uninterrupted business operations, and any security measure that impedes productivity is likely to encounter resistance. In a Zero Trust environment, where every access request is subject to verification, there is a risk that additional friction could slow down workflows or frustrate users. Addressing this challenge requires a delicate balancing act. The strategy must incorporate mechanisms that minimize disruption while still enforcing stringent security controls. This might involve leveraging advanced technologies that enable seamless, background verification processes or designing user interfaces that communicate security protocols transparently without overwhelming the user. Ultimately, the goal is to create a system where robust security measures work in harmony with operational needs, rather than in opposition to them.

The strategic planning for Zero Trust adoption also involves setting clear expectations regarding timelines and resource allocation. Given the complexity of the transformation, it is essential that organizations set realistic deadlines for each phase of the implementation. These timelines should account for the inevitable challenges and delays that arise when integrating new technologies with legacy systems, training staff, and revising policies. Furthermore, resource allocation must be planned carefully, with budgetary provisions made for not only initial investments but also for ongoing maintenance, upgrades, and training. This financial planning is critical because the shift to a Zero Trust model is not a one-time capital expenditure but a continuous investment in the security and resilience of the organization. Decision-makers must view this investment as a necessary part of sustaining business operations in an increasingly hostile digital environment.

Throughout this transformative journey, it is essential to keep the lines of communication open between all parties involved. Regular briefings, progress reports, and feedback sessions create an environment where challenges can be addressed collaboratively, and successes can be celebrated. Such communication helps to break down silos within the organization, ensuring that everyone—from the executive suite to the front-line employees—understands their role in the transformation. It also fosters a culture of transparency and accountability, where the security posture of the organization is seen as a shared responsibility rather than the sole purview of the IT department. By engaging all stakeholders in the process, organizations can build a collective commitment to the principles of Zero Trust, which is essential for long-term success.

Ultimately, planning and strategy for Zero Trust adoption is about more than just implementing new technologies or updating policies. It is about fundamentally rethinking how trust is established and maintained in a digital world where threats are both persistent and evolving. It requires a paradigm shift—a willingness to let go of outdated assumptions about security and embrace a model where verification, accountability, and continuous improvement are paramount. This shift touches every aspect of the organization, from the way systems are designed and integrated to how employees interact with technology on a daily basis. It challenges leaders to look beyond short-term fixes and to invest in a security framework that will stand the test of time.

As organizations navigate the complexities of planning for Zero Trust adoption, they gradually come to understand that this transformation is not merely a defensive measure, but a strategic enabler for the future. In a world where digital threats are increasingly sophisticated and persistent, a robust Zero Trust framework can provide the agility and resilience necessary to sustain competitive advantage. It allows organizations to not only defend against attacks but also to operate with greater confidence in their ability to adapt to new challenges as they arise. In this sense, Zero Trust is not just a security model—it is a strategic asset that supports long-term innovation, growth, and stability.

In conclusion, the planning and strategy phase of Zero Trust adoption is the critical foundation upon which all subsequent efforts are built. It demands a holistic view that encompasses technical assessments, risk analysis, stakeholder engagement, financial planning, and cultural transformation. This phase is marked by careful deliberation, iterative refinement, and a commitment to continuous learning and improvement. While the journey to Zero Trust is complex and fraught with challenges, the benefits—enhanced security, greater operational resilience, and the ability to respond swiftly to emerging threats—are well worth the investment. With a well-crafted roadmap, clear metrics, and a united organizational effort, the transformation to a Zero Trust model becomes not only achievable but a vital step toward securing the digital future in an era of relentless change.

CHAPTER 4: IMPLEMENTING ZERO TRUST – PRACTICAL APPROACHES

Implementing Zero Trust is more than a technical project—it is a comprehensive transformation that reshapes the entire security posture of an organization. As companies move from theory to practice, the transition involves deep changes in technology, culture, and processes that require careful orchestration. At its core, Zero Trust abandons the old adage of "trust but verify" and replaces it with "never trust, always verify," a principle that fundamentally alters how every access request is treated. For instance, a global financial institution that once relied on a secure internal network has restructured its access protocols so that every transaction, whether initiated from a branch office in New York or a remote employee's device in London, is subject to real-time verification.

In the early stages of implementation, organizations must focus on establishing continuous identity verification. Traditional authentication methods, which once relied on static passwords and periodic checks, have given way to a system where verification occurs at every step of the user's interaction with the network. Multi-factor authentication is no longer seen as an optional layer but as a critical baseline. For example, a healthcare provider might require that any doctor accessing patient records must not only enter a password but also verify their identity via a fingerprint scan and a one-time passcode sent to their mobile device. Advanced systems now continuously evaluate behavioral patterns, monitor device health, and assess contextual data such as the time of access and the location of the user. This constant re-validation ensures that even if an attacker breaches the perimeter, they cannot easily move laterally without triggering alerts. The continuous nature of verification creates a dynamic risk profile for each access attempt, allowing the security system to adjust permissions in real time based on emerging threats.

As organizations embark on this transformation, they often face the complex challenge of integrating new security measures with legacy systems that were designed for a static, trusted environment. Many existing infrastructures are built around the idea that once a user is inside the network, they are inherently secure. Transitioning these systems to a Zero Trust model can be daunting. For example, a manufacturing company might operate an older industrial control system that was never designed with modern cybersecurity in mind. In order to secure this system, the company might deploy a virtualized security gateway that sits between the legacy system and the new Zero Trust environment, effectively "translating" outdated protocols into secure, modern transactions. Although this integration can be resource-intensive and complex, the long-term benefits of reducing vulnerabilities and containing potential breaches far outweigh the initial challenges.

Micro-segmentation is another cornerstone of a successful Zero Trust implementation. By dividing the network into many smaller, isolated segments, organizations can limit the potential impact of a breach to a very confined area. In traditional networks, once an attacker penetrated the perimeter, they could often move laterally with ease. In one example, a retail giant reorganized its network so that its payment processing system was completely isolated from its inventory management system. Even if an attacker compromised the inventory segment, they would find it nearly impossible to access the sensitive payment data. This method of compartmentalization forces any intruder to repeatedly prove their trustworthiness with every new access attempt, dramatically reducing the window for exploitation. Implementing micro-segmentation requires a detailed understanding of data flows and the interdependencies between various systems. Over time, as segments are refined and monitored, organizations not only secure their network more effectively but also gain valuable insights into operational inefficiencies and unusual patterns of behavior.

A robust identity and access management (IAM) system is vital in a Zero Trust framework. Rather than granting broad access privileges based solely on a one-time authentication event, modern IAM systems enforce the principle of least privilege continuously. For instance, in a multinational technology firm, employees might be granted access only to the specific project files or applications they need for their role. If an employee who typically works in design suddenly requests access to confidential financial records, the system automatically flags this anomaly and may require additional verification. Every user's access rights are meticulously managed and constantly re-evaluated based on current behavior, context, and risk factors. This dynamic adjustment of privileges, powered by real-time analytics, creates an environment where access is tailored to the user's current situation rather than an assumed level of trust.

Continuous monitoring and advanced analytics are integral to the practical deployment of Zero Trust. Traditional network monitoring often centered around periodic reviews and the analysis of logs that were sometimes hours or even days old. In a Zero Trust environment, every transaction, data exchange, and access attempt is scrutinized in real time. Consider an e-commerce company that processes millions of transactions daily; implementing continuous monitoring allows its security team to detect unusual patterns, such as a sudden surge in failed login attempts from a particular region, and respond immediately. This requires a sophisticated infrastructure that can process vast amounts of data without introducing significant latency into the user experience. Artificial intelligence and machine learning play crucial roles in this context by establishing baselines for normal activity, detecting subtle deviations, and identifying potential threats before they escalate into full-blown incidents. The integration of AI-driven analytics not only enhances the speed and accuracy of threat detection but also assists in automating responses. For example, if an anomalous pattern is detected in one segment of the network, the system might automatically isolate that segment while alerting security teams, thereby containing the threat swiftly and effectively.

Implementing Zero Trust in today's complex digital environments also demands a rethinking of policies and governance structures. Security policies that were once static and rigid must evolve into dynamic guidelines that can adjust to real-time risk assessments. Organizations are now drafting policies that are not only comprehensive but also flexible enough to adapt to evolving threats. For instance, a global logistics company may update its access policies based on the time of day and the current threat level in a particular region, ensuring that remote drivers accessing sensitive data are subject to additional verification when operating in high-risk areas. These policies outline the specific criteria under which access is granted, the circumstances that necessitate re-authentication, and the protocols for responding to detected anomalies. Crafting these policies is often a collaborative process involving IT, legal, compliance, and human resources. The goal is to create a living framework that governs every interaction while accommodating the rapidly changing landscape of cybersecurity threats. This collaborative approach helps ensure that the policies are both technically sound and practically implementable, aligning with the broader objectives of the organization.

One of the major challenges in implementing Zero Trust is finding the right balance between robust security measures and user convenience. Introducing stringent access controls and continuous verification processes can sometimes create friction in daily operations. For example, a software company might initially see pushback from its development teams if multi-factor authentication delays their workflow. To mitigate this, organizations are investing in technologies that streamline the authentication process. Single sign-on solutions combined with behavioral biometrics can provide a seamless yet secure experience, reducing the perceived burden on users. The key is to design a system that operates largely in the background, making security checks as unobtrusive as possible while maintaining a high level of vigilance. Over time, as users become familiar with these processes and see the tangible benefits of enhanced security, acceptance tends to grow. Organizations that manage this balance effectively often report that their employees become active participants in maintaining security, rather than viewing it as an external imposition.

Training and cultural transformation are also critical components of the Zero Trust implementation process. The technical measures can only be as effective as the people who operate and support them. For example, a regional bank may launch a series of interactive training workshops where employees simulate phishing attacks and unauthorized access scenarios, demonstrating the importance of following new protocols. Such initiatives help embed a security-first mindset throughout the organization. Comprehensive training programs that cover both the technical aspects and the underlying philosophy of continuous verification and adaptive security help demystify the technology. Workshops, simulations, and regular briefings ensure that every member of the organization, from executives to front-line employees, understands their role in maintaining a secure environment. As employees become more aware of the evolving nature of cyber threats and the necessity of these measures, they are more likely to comply with the new protocols and even contribute to ongoing improvements.

Another significant aspect of the practical implementation of

Zero Trust is the development of a robust incident response strategy. The Zero Trust model operates on the assumption that breaches are not a matter of if, but when. Therefore, organizations must be prepared for inevitable security incidents by developing comprehensive response plans that leverage the granular control and monitoring inherent in a Zero Trust environment. For instance, when a major telecommunications company experienced a breach in one of its segments, its pre-established incident response playbook enabled it to immediately isolate the affected area and launch a targeted investigation, preventing the breach from spreading further. Detailed playbooks outline the steps to be taken when a breach is detected, including the immediate isolation of affected segments, the activation of additional authentication measures, and clear communication protocols for both internal teams and external stakeholders. Regular drills and simulations ensure that the incident response team remains well-practiced and ready to act decisively, reducing the potential damage and downtime in the event of a real attack.

Cloud environments and the integration of remote work further complicate the implementation of Zero Trust, but they also underscore its necessity. As more organizations move critical functions to cloud platforms and employees work from diverse locations, the traditional network perimeter becomes even more obsolete. For example, a multinational consulting firm with offices across different continents and a significant number of remote workers must ensure that whether an employee is accessing the company's CRM from a home office in Berlin or a client site in Singapore, the same rigorous security checks are applied. This requires the deployment of unified security platforms that can enforce consistent policies across hybrid environments. The challenge lies in integrating disparate systems and ensuring that the same high standards of verification are applied regardless of where the data or application resides. Successful implementations often involve close collaboration with cloud service providers and the adoption of API-driven security solutions that can bridge the gap between on-premises and cloud-based infrastructures. By maintaining a unified security posture, organizations can ensure that every access point, whether physical or virtual, is subject to the same rigorous verification protocols.

In practical terms, the journey to full Zero Trust implementation is iterative and evolutionary. Organizations typically start with pilot projects that focus on the most critical areas of the network. For instance, a regional energy provider might pilot Zero Trust principles in its critical infrastructure systems before rolling them out to administrative networks. These pilots serve as testing grounds for new technologies, policies, and processes, allowing security teams to gather valuable data and refine their approaches before scaling the solution enterprise-wide. Early successes provide tangible evidence of the benefits of Zero Trust and help build momentum for broader adoption. Each phase of the implementation brings with it lessons that are integrated into subsequent stages, fostering a culture of continuous improvement. The iterative nature of the process is one of its greatest strengths, as it allows organizations to adapt to new threats and emerging technologies without overhauling their entire security framework in one fell swoop.

The expanded scope of Zero Trust implementation also involves the integration of advanced threat intelligence. By connecting the security system to external intelligence feeds and internal data repositories, organizations can gain real-time insights into the evolving threat landscape. For example, a logistics company might integrate threat intelligence from global cybersecurity agencies, allowing its systems to automatically adjust access protocols when a new vulnerability is identified in commonly used software. This intelligence is used to dynamically adjust security policies, prioritize alerts, and focus resources on the most pressing risks. The feedback loop created by continuous monitoring, automated threat detection, and real-time intelligence ensures that the security framework remains both proactive and responsive.

Ultimately, the practical implementation of Zero Trust is not merely about deploying new technologies, but about fundamentally rethinking the relationship between users, devices, and data in a digital environment. It is a comprehensive approach that requires investment in technology, processes, and people, all aligned towards the common goal of creating a secure, resilient, and adaptive organization. As organizations continue on this path, they not only improve their ability to defend against cyber threats but also gain a strategic advantage in an increasingly competitive digital marketplace. By embracing a model where security is woven into every interaction and continuously validated, they lay the groundwork for a future where digital trust is earned rather than assumed.

Through careful planning, methodical implementation, and ongoing adaptation, the Zero Trust model becomes not just a set of technical measures, but a strategic framework that redefines how organizations operate in the digital age. It is a transformative approach that turns every access attempt into a moment of verification, every system interaction into a checkpoint for security, and every potential vulnerability into an opportunity for improvement. In embracing this paradigm, organizations take a decisive step towards a future where security is not just a barrier against threats, but a foundation for innovation, efficiency, and enduring trust in a constantly evolving digital world.

CHAPTER 5: TECHNOLOGIES AND TOOLS FOR ZERO TRUST

The journey toward Zero Trust is as much about adopting the right technologies and tools as it is about redefining security philosophy. In today's complex digital landscape, the implementation of Zero Trust principles relies on an array of innovative solutions that transform abstract concepts into tangible, actionable defenses. The transformation is not simply a matter of adding new software or hardware but of reimagining the entire technological ecosystem in a way that makes every interaction a potential checkpoint for security. Over the past decade, the emergence of technologies such as software-defined perimeters, advanced cloud security solutions, and cutting-edge artificial intelligence has fundamentally reshaped how organizations secure their digital assets, enabling a transition from static defenses to dynamic, adaptive systems.

One of the foundational components of a Zero Trust infrastructure is the concept of the software-defined perimeter. Traditional network designs once relied on rigid perimeters—firewalls, virtual private networks, and other hardware-based defenses—that were intended to keep intruders out of a trusted zone. However, as organizations have become more distributed and interconnected, these perimeters have dissolved, leaving behind gaps that attackers can exploit. The software-defined perimeter, by contrast, takes a different approach. Instead of relying on physical boundaries, it creates virtual boundaries that are dynamically defined based on user identity, device posture, and contextual risk. For example, a multinational corporation might use a software-defined perimeter to restrict access to sensitive financial systems. Employees attempting to log in from an unusual location or with an unrecognized device are challenged with additional authentication steps or may even be denied access entirely. In one real-world case, a global logistics provider was able to segment its operational network so finely that when a breach was attempted from an external source, the attacker found themselves confined to a single, isolated segment with no lateral movement possible. This approach not only limits the damage that any single breach can cause but also provides detailed telemetry on every access attempt, turning potential points of vulnerability into opportunities for continuous monitoring and improvement.

As organizations increasingly migrate their data and applications to the cloud, the need for robust cloud security solutions that align with Zero Trust principles becomes paramount. The cloud presents unique challenges because it is inherently borderless; data flows freely between on-premises systems and various cloud services, and employees can access corporate resources from virtually anywhere in the world. To secure this environment, companies are turning to cloud-native security tools that enforce Zero Trust policies across all platforms. For instance, a leading healthcare organization adopted a cloud security solution that integrated with its electronic health record system. The tool continuously monitored access attempts across multiple cloud environments, analyzing behavior patterns and contextual data to ensure that only authenticated and authorized users could access patient data. When the system detected an anomalous pattern —such as a sudden surge in data requests from a remote location—it automatically isolated the activity and triggered an investigation. By applying Zero Trust principles to cloud security, organizations can maintain a consistent security posture regardless of where their data resides, ensuring that every access attempt is scrutinized with the same rigor as if it were occurring on a traditional corporate network.

Emerging technologies play an equally vital role in enabling Zero Trust. Artificial intelligence and machine learning, for example, have revolutionized the way security teams detect and respond to threats. These technologies analyze enormous volumes of data in real time, identifying subtle patterns and deviations from the norm that might indicate a potential breach. In one instance, a financial services firm integrated AI-driven analytics into its security operations. The system learned over time what constituted normal behavior for its users and endpoints, and when it detected even a minor deviation— such as an employee accessing sensitive files at odd hours or from a location inconsistent with their typical behavior —it automatically initiated additional verification protocols. In another case, a retail company used machine learning to monitor customer interactions on its e-commerce platform, ensuring that transactions flagged for unusual behavior were promptly reviewed by security analysts. The result was a system that not only reduced the incidence of false alarms but also improved the speed and accuracy of threat detection, allowing the organization to address potential breaches before they escalated.

Beyond these high-level technologies, there is a suite of specialized tools designed to implement the granular aspects of Zero Trust. Identity and access management solutions have evolved from static, one-time authentication systems into dynamic platforms that continuously evaluate risk. Modern IAM tools integrate biometric authentication, risk-based authentication, and adaptive access control into a unified framework. Consider the example of a technology startup that adopted an advanced IAM solution which required employees to re-authenticate periodically throughout the day. The system tracked behavioral indicators such as typing patterns, navigation habits, and even mouse movements. When a user deviated from their established pattern, the system prompted additional security checks before granting further access. This not only strengthened the overall security posture but also provided the IT team with a wealth of behavioral data that could be used to fine-tune access policies.

Another crucial tool in the Zero Trust arsenal is network segmentation. While the concept of micro-segmentation has been discussed as a theoretical pillar of Zero Trust, its practical implementation requires sophisticated software and orchestration tools. In one illustrative case, a government agency responsible for sensitive national security data implemented a micro-segmentation strategy that divided its network into dozens of isolated segments. Each segment was governed by its own set of policies, ensuring that if one segment were breached, the attacker would encounter multiple layers of defense before gaining access to any critical data. Tools that automate the segmentation process, monitor inter-segment traffic, and enforce access controls on a granular level were essential in achieving this objective. The result was a network that was not only more secure but also more manageable, with clear insights into data flows and potential vulnerabilities.

Automation and orchestration tools further enhance the practical implementation of Zero Trust. In a modern security environment, the volume of data and the speed at which threats emerge can overwhelm even the most experienced human analysts. Automation allows routine tasks—such as patch management, log analysis, and threat response—to be carried out swiftly and accurately without human intervention. For example, a large telecommunications company deployed an orchestration platform that integrated its various security tools. When the system detected an anomaly, the orchestration platform automatically isolated the affected segment, applied necessary patches, and notified the relevant teams, all within a matter of seconds. This rapid response capability is critical in a Zero Trust model, where the assumption is that breaches are inevitable and must be contained immediately to prevent widespread damage.

Encryption and data protection technologies are also integral to Zero Trust. In a world where data is constantly in motion—

across devices, networks, and cloud environments—the ability to protect data both at rest and in transit is paramount. Advanced encryption algorithms, combined with dynamic key management systems, ensure that even if data is intercepted, it remains unreadable to unauthorized parties. For example, an international energy company implemented end-to-end encryption for all its communications, both internally and with external partners. The system dynamically adjusted encryption parameters based on the sensitivity of the data and the risk level of the access request. This level of granular control over data protection is essential in a Zero Trust model, where every data transaction is a potential target for attackers.

The rise of the Internet of Things (IoT) has introduced an entirely new set of challenges and opportunities for Zero Trust. With millions of devices—from industrial sensors to smart appliances—connecting to corporate networks, ensuring that each device meets security standards becomes a monumental task. IoT security platforms have emerged that are specifically designed to monitor and control the behavior of these devices. For example, a manufacturing plant deployed an IoT security solution that continuously monitored the performance and behavior of its automated production lines. When a sensor or device exhibited abnormal behavior, the system automatically isolated it from the rest of the network until it could be inspected by security personnel. This proactive approach not only prevents potential breaches but also maintains the integrity and reliability of critical operational systems.

A critical trend accelerating the adoption of Zero Trust is the increasing prevalence of edge computing. In traditional models, security was centralized in data centers; today, processing power is distributed closer to where data is generated. For instance, a large retail chain with stores across the country might use edge computing devices to manage in-store operations. Integrating Zero Trust at the edge ensures that each device—from point-of-sale systems to digital signage—is subject to continuous verification and monitoring. This decentralized approach minimizes the risk of widespread breaches by ensuring that even if one edge device is compromised, the breach does not extend to the entire network.

Another emerging area is the convergence of Zero Trust with blockchain technology. Blockchain's decentralized and immutable ledger can provide robust identity management and secure logging. For example, a pioneering project at a major financial institution explored using blockchain to create an indelible record of every access attempt made across the network. This record not only enhanced transparency and accountability but also made it significantly more challenging for attackers to cover their tracks. While still in the experimental stage for many organizations, blockchain holds promise for further reinforcing the principles of Zero Trust by providing a secure, verifiable audit trail for all interactions.

The integration of these diverse technologies into a cohesive Zero Trust framework requires careful planning and coordination. Organizations must choose tools that not only fulfill individual roles but also communicate effectively with each other to create a unified defense system. Interoperability becomes as important as individual capability. Many organizations are now moving toward integrated security platforms that combine IAM, network segmentation, continuous monitoring, and threat intelligence into a single pane of glass. For instance, a global retail chain implemented an integrated security solution that provided real-time visibility into every access attempt, every data flow, and every endpoint's status. This unified view allowed the security team to quickly correlate data from different sources, identify potential threats, and take decisive action. The integrated approach not only streamlined operations but also enhanced the overall security posture by ensuring that no aspect of the network was left unmonitored or unprotected.

Vendors and technology providers have recognized the growing demand for Zero Trust solutions and are continuously innovating to meet the needs of modern enterprises. Many leading providers now offer Zero Trust as a service, enabling organizations to adopt the model without the need for extensive in-house infrastructure. For example, a midsize financial firm partnered with a prominent security vendor that provided a cloud-based Zero Trust platform. This platform delivered continuous identity verification, real-time threat analytics, and automated incident response capabilities through a subscription model. The firm was able to implement a comprehensive Zero Trust strategy without the upfront costs of building a dedicated infrastructure from scratch, illustrating how vendor solutions can democratize access to advanced security measures.

The evolution of technology also means that the tools available today are likely to be supplanted by even more advanced solutions in the future. As quantum computing, blockchain, and other disruptive technologies mature, they are expected to further reshape the cybersecurity landscape. Researchers are already exploring how quantum-resistant encryption and blockchain-based identity management systems can provide even greater levels of assurance in a Zero Trust environment. For instance, a pioneering research project at a leading university is testing blockchain as a means to create immutable logs of every access request, ensuring that all actions within a network are permanently recorded and verifiable. Such innovations have the potential to add an additional layer of security and trust, ensuring that the Zero Trust model remains robust even in the face of future technological challenges.

The practical adoption of Zero Trust technologies is also deeply intertwined with compliance and regulatory requirements. Industries such as healthcare, finance, and government are subject to stringent data protection regulations, and the granular, continuous monitoring offered by Zero Trust can help organizations meet these requirements more effectively. For example, a healthcare organization might leverage a Zero Trust framework to ensure compliance with HIPAA by continuously monitoring access to patient records and generating real-time reports that demonstrate adherence to privacy standards. Similarly, a European bank can use Zero Trust principles to support GDPR compliance by ensuring that data access is tightly controlled and auditable, reducing the risk of unauthorized exposure.

Integration with broader security frameworks is another important consideration. Many organizations are deploying Security Information and Event Management (SIEM) systems and Security Orchestration, Automation, and Response (SOAR) platforms that work in tandem with Zero Trust tools. These systems collect and analyze security events across the entire enterprise, providing a holistic view of the security landscape. For example, when a Zero Trust system flags an unusual access attempt, the SIEM can correlate that event with other data points—such as a spike in network traffic or known indicators of compromise—to provide a more complete picture of potential threats. The SOAR platform then automates the response, triggering predefined workflows that help contain the incident. This integration of Zero Trust with existing security infrastructure ensures that organizations are not working in silos but are instead leveraging every available resource to protect their digital assets.

Furthermore, as organizations deploy these advanced technologies, they are also investing in training and continuous improvement programs. Security teams participate in regular workshops, simulations, and tabletop exercises designed to test and refine the Zero Trust infrastructure. These exercises often reveal gaps in the system and provide invaluable feedback that drives further innovation. For instance, a major telecommunications company conducted a series of simulated cyberattacks on its Zero Trust system. The lessons learned from these exercises led to enhancements in its orchestration platform and adjustments in its micro-segmentation strategies, ultimately resulting in a more robust and resilient security posture.

Another dimension that has emerged in recent years is the importance of real-time risk scoring. Some advanced Zero Trust platforms now assign a dynamic risk score to every user and device, which is recalculated continuously based on factors such as behavior, device health, and contextual data. A multinational enterprise might use such a system to determine that an employee's risk score has increased due to abnormal login patterns from an unusual location, prompting the system to require additional verification before granting access. This real-time risk scoring not only enhances security but also provides management with clear, quantifiable metrics that can inform broader risk management strategies and policy adjustments.

In summary, the technologies and tools that underpin Zero Trust are not just isolated components—they are interconnected parts of a larger ecosystem designed to create a dynamic, adaptive, and resilient security posture. By integrating software-defined perimeters, cloud-native security solutions, AI-driven analytics, advanced IAM, micro-segmentation, orchestration platforms, encryption technologies, IoT security solutions, and emerging innovations such as blockchain and quantum-resistant encryption, organizations build a defense system that is both comprehensive and flexible. This ecosystem empowers enterprises to verify every interaction, continuously monitor every access request, and rapidly respond to potential threats—all while maintaining compliance with regulatory standards and adapting to an ever-evolving threat landscape.

As the digital world continues to expand and evolve, so too will the tools and technologies that support the Zero Trust model. Organizations that invest in these technologies not only protect themselves against current threats but also lay the foundation for a future where security is proactive, adaptive, and deeply integrated into every facet of their operations. In doing so, they turn every challenge into an opportunity, ensuring that trust is not simply granted by default, but earned continuously through rigorous, real-time verification processes.

CHAPTER 6: CASE STUDIES AND BEST PRACTICES

In the ever-shifting landscape of cybersecurity, the theoretical underpinnings of Zero Trust are best understood through the lens of real-world application. This chapter delves deeply into a range of case studies and best practices that illustrate how organizations across diverse industries have successfully adopted and adapted Zero Trust principles. By examining detailed narratives of healthcare institutions, financial services firms, government agencies, global retailers, manufacturing plants, and even technology startups, we see that the journey toward Zero Trust is as much about cultural transformation and organizational strategy as it is about deploying advanced technologies.

One of the earliest and most compelling examples comes from the healthcare sector, where the stakes for data security are extraordinarily high. A leading healthcare organization, burdened by the legacy of outdated perimeter-based defenses, faced a growing number of cyberattacks that threatened patient records and critical clinical data. In response, the organization initiated a comprehensive Zero Trust transformation. Instead of relying on a traditional network boundary to protect sensitive information, every request to access electronic health records was reimagined as a potential threat. For instance, a physician attempting to retrieve patient data from a hospital workstation would not simply be granted access based on an initial login. Instead, the system continuously evaluated contextual factors such as the device's security posture, the physical location of the request, and even the time of day. If a doctor's request was made from an unfamiliar terminal or outside of normal operating hours, the system would trigger additional authentication steps

—ranging from biometric scans to one-time passcodes sent to a verified mobile device. Over a period of eighteen months, this rigorous approach resulted in a dramatic reduction in unauthorized access incidents. Not only did the system prevent breaches, but it also provided granular logs and real-time alerts that allowed the organization to fine-tune its security policies. The healthcare provider's success was attributed to the seamless integration of continuous monitoring, adaptive authentication protocols, and a culture of security awareness that permeated every level of the organization.

In the financial services sector, a global firm with a sprawling network of trading platforms and customer service centers embarked on a Zero Trust journey following a series of high-profile phishing attacks and internal breaches. Historically, the firm had operated under the assumption that internal network traffic was inherently safe, a mindset that proved disastrously outdated. The transformation began with a complete audit of all user accounts, data flows, and access privileges. This audit led to the deployment of a state-of-the-art identity and access management (IAM) system that enforced the principle of least privilege. For example, traders working on the front lines were given access solely to the applications necessary for their trading activities, while sensitive functions such as financial reporting and risk management were strictly compartmentalized. The system continuously recalculated risk scores for each user based on behavior analytics; an employee who suddenly deviated from their usual login pattern—perhaps by accessing the system from a new geographic location—would have their risk profile adjusted in real time, triggering further verification. One illustrative incident involved a trader whose account was compromised after a phishing scam. The Zero Trust system detected unusual patterns in the account's activity and promptly locked it down, forcing an immediate review by the security team. This swift action not only mitigated the damage but also provided invaluable insights into the evolving tactics of cybercriminals. As a result, the firm reported a significant decrease in both the number and severity of security incidents, along with improved regulatory compliance and stronger customer trust.

Government agencies, which often deal with some of the most sensitive data in the public domain, have also embraced Zero Trust with remarkable success. A prominent agency responsible for national security and intelligence undertook a pilot program to retrofit its aging IT infrastructure with Zero Trust principles. The agency's legacy systems were a mosaic of outdated technologies interwoven with modern applications, presenting a formidable challenge. To address this, the agency deployed a software-defined perimeter (SDP) solution that created dynamic, virtual boundaries around critical data repositories. Every attempt to access classified information was subject to rigorous contextual analysis, including the assessment of device integrity, user credentials, and even environmental factors such as whether the access request originated from within a secure government facility or from an unsecured public network. During one noteworthy incident, a series of access attempts from an overseas location were immediately flagged by the SDP system. The system automatically isolated the affected segment, allowing security teams to investigate without exposing the broader network. This proactive incident response not only thwarted a potential breach but also reinforced the agency's overall confidence in its new Zero Trust framework. Best practices emerging from this case emphasized the need for tight integration between real-time threat intelligence and the granular control provided by software-defined perimeters, as well as the critical importance of ongoing training and policy refinement.

A global retailer, managing thousands of brick-and-mortar stores alongside a burgeoning e-commerce platform, offers another illustrative case study. The retailer had long struggled with the challenge of securing an extensive, hybrid environment that spanned physical storefronts, centralized data centers, and cloud-based services. Recognizing the limitations of a traditional network security model, the retailer embarked on a comprehensive Zero Trust initiative that unified its security posture across all operational domains. In this transformation, every access attempt—whether by a store manager using a mobile device or an online customer service representative accessing customer data—was subject to continuous verification. For example, when an employee attempted to access sensitive customer information from an unfamiliar device or from an offsite location, the system would automatically require multi-factor authentication and, in some cases, temporarily restrict access until further verification was completed. The integrated security platform employed by the retailer offered real-time visibility into every transaction, enabling the security team to correlate data from various sources and identify emerging threats quickly. Over the course of two years, the retailer not only reduced its incidence of data breaches but also discovered unexpected operational benefits; the unified security system provided analytics that helped optimize supply chain logistics and improve customer experience. This case reinforces the best practice of aligning security initiatives with overall business objectives, ensuring that robust protection measures can also drive innovation and efficiency.

Manufacturing companies face their own unique challenges when it comes to cybersecurity, particularly as they integrate operational technology (OT) and a growing array of Internet of Things (IoT) devices into their networks. One manufacturing plant, for instance, embarked on a Zero Trust transformation to secure its production line, which had become increasingly connected to the corporate network for real-time performance monitoring. Historically, the plant operated under the assumption that the internal network was a safe space for critical control systems. However, with cyber threats evolving to target industrial control systems, management recognized the need to treat every access point as a potential risk. They implemented a micro-segmentation strategy that isolated OT systems from the broader IT network, ensuring that any breach in the IT domain would not compromise the production line. In addition, IoT security platforms were deployed to continuously monitor the behavior of connected devices—such as sensors, actuators, and robotic systems. When a sensor began transmitting data outside of its normal parameters, the system automatically isolated it from the rest of the network pending further inspection. This approach not only minimized the potential impact of a cyberattack but also improved the reliability of the production process. The manufacturing plant's experience underlines the importance of tailored Zero Trust implementations that account for the specific risks and operational characteristics of industrial environments.

Smaller organizations and startups have also found value in the Zero Trust model, even though they may not have the extensive resources of larger enterprises. A technology startup specializing in software development, for example, implemented a Zero Trust framework early in its growth to protect its intellectual property and customer data. With a nimble, agile workforce spread across different regions, the startup recognized that its distributed nature required a modern security approach. By adopting cloud-based identity and access management tools, the company ensured that every code repository, development environment, and customer database was protected by continuous verification protocols. When an employee attempted to access the company's development platform from a new location or using an unrecognized device, the system would automatically prompt for additional verification steps. This proactive stance not only safeguarded the startup's valuable assets but also built a culture of security among its employees, who came to view each access attempt as an opportunity to contribute to the company's overall defense. This example illustrates a best practice for small and medium enterprises: even with limited resources, investing in scalable, cloud-based Zero Trust solutions can yield significant security benefits and foster a security-first mindset across the organization.

Beyond these individual case studies, several overarching best practices have emerged that can guide any organization considering a transition to Zero Trust. One of the most critical lessons is the importance of conducting a comprehensive assessment of the existing security landscape. Organizations that succeed in implementing Zero Trust begin by meticulously mapping out their assets, data flows, user interactions, and potential vulnerabilities. This detailed understanding serves as the foundation upon which a tailored Zero Trust strategy is built. Next, continuous monitoring is not just a technical requirement but a strategic imperative. The deployment of real-time analytics and machine learning tools to evaluate every access attempt and transaction enables organizations to detect anomalies as they occur and adjust their defenses accordingly. This dynamic approach is in stark contrast to static, periodic reviews that can leave critical gaps in security.

Integration is another key theme. Many organizations operate in transitional states where legacy systems must coexist with modern applications. A best practice in this context is to adopt intermediary solutions—such as virtualized gateways or custom APIs—that allow older systems to interface securely with newer, Zero Trust-compliant technologies. This incremental approach not only protects existing investments but also paves the way for gradual modernization without disrupting ongoing operations. Equally important is the emphasis on user education and cultural change. No technological solution can succeed without the support and understanding of the people who use it. Regular training sessions, simulated cyberattacks, and cross-departmental collaboration help embed a security-first mindset that is essential for the success of any Zero Trust initiative. When every employee understands their role in maintaining security—from recognizing phishing attempts to adhering to strict access protocols—the entire organization becomes a more robust defender against cyber threats.

Incident response strategies, too, are a cornerstone of effective Zero Trust implementations. Given that no system can guarantee absolute security, organizations must be prepared for breaches by developing detailed incident response plans that leverage the granular visibility offered by Zero Trust tools. These plans should include predefined workflows for isolating affected segments, conducting forensic analysis, and communicating with stakeholders. Regular drills and simulations help ensure that when an incident does occur, the response is swift, coordinated, and effective. A government agency's experience with a coordinated cyber-espionage attempt underscores the importance of having a robust, practiced incident response strategy that can contain threats before they escalate.

The financial benefits of adopting Zero Trust, while often secondary to the imperative of enhanced security, are also significant. Improved data visibility and risk management can lead to cost savings in terms of reduced breach incidents, lower regulatory fines, and increased operational efficiency. For example, the global retailer that unified its security across physical and digital domains not only strengthened its defenses but also gained insights that improved supply chain management and customer service. These operational benefits demonstrate that Zero Trust is not merely a defensive posture but a strategic asset that can drive overall business performance.

Moreover, as organizations continue to iterate on their Zero Trust implementations, they often find that the process itself drives innovation. The continuous feedback loops created by real-time monitoring and dynamic risk assessment lead to ongoing refinements in both technology and policy. A manufacturing plant, for instance, used insights from its IoT security platform not only to prevent breaches but also to optimize its production processes by identifying inefficiencies and abnormal device behaviors. This iterative cycle of improvement creates a self-reinforcing ecosystem where security enhancements lead to operational insights, which in turn inform further security innovations.

Another dimension to consider is the role of external partnerships and vendor ecosystems in the Zero Trust journey. Many organizations have found that collaborating with specialized security vendors—who offer solutions as a service or through integrated platforms—can accelerate the transition to a robust Zero Trust model. A midsize financial firm, for instance, partnered with a leading security vendor to implement a cloud-based Zero Trust platform. This partnership allowed the firm to leverage state-of-the-art identity verification, real-time threat analytics, and automated response capabilities without the significant upfront costs and complexity of developing an in-house solution. Such collaborations not only democratize access to advanced security technologies but also enable organizations to stay abreast of the latest innovations in the field.

Perhaps one of the most enduring lessons from these case studies is that the journey to Zero Trust is not a one-time project but a continuous evolution. Cyber threats are constantly evolving, and as they do, so too must the defenses that protect against them. Organizations that view Zero Trust as an ongoing process—rather than a finished state—are better positioned to adapt to emerging risks and incorporate new technologies as they become available. This mindset of perpetual improvement is essential for maintaining resilience in a digital world where change is the only constant.

In conclusion, the case studies and best practices presented in this chapter demonstrate that the successful implementation of Zero Trust is characterized by a multifaceted approach. It requires a deep understanding of the existing security landscape, continuous monitoring and dynamic risk assessment, seamless integration of both legacy and modern systems, a strong culture of user education and collaboration, robust incident response strategies, and strategic partnerships with leading technology vendors. Each real-world example —from healthcare providers and financial institutions to government agencies, retailers, manufacturers, and startups— offers unique insights into how Zero Trust can be tailored to meet the specific challenges of different industries. These narratives reinforce the idea that Zero Trust is not a static set of rules but a living, evolving framework that continuously adapts to the threat landscape while also driving operational efficiency and business innovation.

The journey to Zero Trust, as chronicled in these case studies, is a testament to the power of rethinking traditional security paradigms. By transforming every access attempt into a moment of verification, every system interaction into a checkpoint for security, and every potential vulnerability into an opportunity for improvement, organizations are redefining what it means to protect data in the digital age. In doing so, they not only mitigate the risks posed by increasingly sophisticated cyber threats but also lay the foundation for a future where trust is continuously earned and reinforced through rigorous, real-time validation processes.

As more organizations share their experiences and refine their approaches, the collective wisdom of these efforts will continue to shape the evolution of cybersecurity. The lessons learned here serve as a roadmap for any enterprise willing to embrace a paradigm shift—a roadmap that moves from static defenses toward a dynamic, adaptive, and ultimately more resilient model of security. In this new landscape, Zero Trust is not merely a defensive strategy; it is a strategic asset that drives innovation, improves operational efficiency, and ultimately secures the digital future.

The transformation is challenging, yet the rewards are profound. Organizations that fully embrace Zero Trust enjoy not only a lower incidence of breaches and faster incident response times but also the intangible benefits of enhanced trust from their customers, partners, and regulators. In a world where data is the currency of commerce and cyber threats are an ever-present risk, the case for Zero Trust becomes undeniable. The journey may be long and fraught with obstacles, but the outcome—a secure, agile, and future-proof digital ecosystem—is worth every step taken along the way.

Ultimately, the narratives presented in this chapter reinforce a simple yet profound truth: in the realm of cybersecurity, the only constant is change, and the only way to stay ahead is to embrace a model that is as dynamic as the threats it seeks to counter. Zero Trust, as demonstrated through these diverse case studies and best practices, is not just a set of technical solutions; it is a transformative approach that redefines trust, drives continuous improvement, and secures the digital landscapes upon which modern society depends.

CHAPTER 7: ZERO TRUST IN THE ERA OF REMOTE WORK AND IOT

In today's digital landscape, the traditional boundaries of the corporate network are rapidly dissolving. The rise of remote work and the explosion of Internet of Things (IoT) devices have created an environment where employees and devices access corporate resources from countless locations and through diverse channels. This evolution demands that organizations rethink how trust is established and maintained. Zero Trust, as a security paradigm, is uniquely suited to address these challenges by enforcing continuous verification and granular access control for every user, device, and application regardless of location. This chapter explores the transformative impact of remote work and IoT on cybersecurity and examines how Zero Trust principles can be applied to secure a distributed, interconnected environment.

The shift to remote work was accelerated by global events and has fundamentally altered the traditional office model. Employees now routinely work from home, co-working spaces, or while traveling. In this new paradigm, the secure corporate perimeter has virtually vanished. Instead of being contained within a fortified network, employees access sensitive systems from networks that are not under the direct control of the organization. This raises significant security challenges, as home networks, public Wi-Fi, and mobile data connections may be inherently less secure. Zero Trust addresses these challenges by rejecting the notion of inherent trust based on location. Every access request—whether it originates from the company headquarters or a remote coffee shop—is treated with equal suspicion until it can be verified through rigorous, continuous authentication and contextual analysis.

For example, consider a multinational consulting firm that has shifted to a fully remote work model. In the past, employees accessed secure internal systems from a controlled office environment where network traffic was monitored and endpoints managed by the IT department. Today, the same employees might log in from home networks that vary in security, or from shared spaces where the risk of eavesdropping is high. By implementing Zero Trust, the firm has reconfigured its access protocols so that each login triggers multi-factor authentication. Beyond just a password and a one-time code, the system also monitors device health, browser behavior, and even geolocation data. If an employee's login attempt originates from an unusual location or from a device that hasn't been updated with the latest security patches, the system automatically applies stricter controls or delays access until further verification is completed. In one instance, an employee attempted to access confidential client data from a public Wi-Fi network at an airport. The Zero Trust system flagged the request as high risk due to the combination of location and untrusted network conditions, and it automatically routed the access through a secure virtual private network (VPN) while prompting the user for additional verification. This layered approach not only protects sensitive data but also educates employees about the importance of secure practices.

Remote work environments also require a significant transformation in endpoint management. In a traditional office, corporate devices are typically managed centrally, with standardized configurations and regular security updates. In contrast, remote workers often use a mix of corporate-issued laptops, personal devices, and even mobile phones. Each device represents a potential vulnerability if not properly secured. Zero Trust extends beyond the network to the endpoints, mandating that each device's security posture be continuously assessed. This is achieved by integrating endpoint detection and response (EDR) solutions that monitor for signs of compromise, enforce encryption, and ensure that antivirus and firewall protections are active and up-to-date. For instance, a large software development company implemented an EDR solution across all devices accessing its development environment. The system automatically quarantined any device that exhibited suspicious behavior, such as unusual file modifications or unexpected network connections, and it prompted the security team to investigate. As a result, the company significantly reduced the risk of malware propagation and unauthorized access, demonstrating the effectiveness of a Zero Trust approach in a remote work context.

The transformation brought about by remote work is not solely a technical challenge—it also requires a cultural shift within the organization. Employees must be educated about the risks associated with remote access and the rationale behind continuous verification. Training programs and regular security awareness sessions help to foster a mindset where every access attempt is understood as a potential risk that needs to be verified. When employees understand that the strict security measures are not intended to hinder their work but to protect both personal and corporate data, they become more cooperative and proactive in maintaining security hygiene. This cultural change is essential, as the human factor often represents the weakest link in cybersecurity. In many organizations that have successfully embraced Zero Trust, employees have come to view additional authentication steps and continuous monitoring as necessary measures that safeguard their work and personal information alike.

While remote work poses significant challenges, the proliferation of IoT devices adds an even more complex layer to the security landscape. The IoT revolution has brought connectivity to everyday objects, from industrial sensors and smart appliances to wearable health monitors and home security systems. In many cases, these devices operate with minimal security measures and are deployed in vast numbers, making them attractive targets for attackers. An attacker who compromises a single IoT device can potentially use it as a foothold to infiltrate broader networks, launch distributed denial-of-service (DDoS) attacks, or exfiltrate sensitive data.

IoT devices often operate on minimal operating systems, with limited computing power and storage, and they sometimes lack the robust security controls found in more sophisticated endpoints. This makes it challenging to deploy traditional security solutions. Zero Trust offers a solution by insisting that every device, no matter how small or seemingly insignificant, must continuously prove its identity and security posture before being granted access to sensitive resources. For example, a smart city initiative in a large metropolitan area sought to interconnect traffic sensors, surveillance cameras, and environmental monitors to improve urban planning and public safety. However, the city's IT department quickly realized that without a Zero Trust framework, these devices could serve as entry points for cyberattacks. By segmenting the network and enforcing continuous verification on each IoT device, the city was able to ensure that even if one sensor was compromised, the breach would not spread to critical systems such as the traffic control center or emergency services. Each device was assigned a unique identity, and its behavior was continuously monitored for anomalies. If a device began communicating outside of its expected parameters—for instance, if a temperature sensor in a public park started transmitting data at unusually high frequencies—it would trigger an automatic investigation, and the device's network access would be temporarily suspended. This approach not only improved the security of the IoT network but also provided the city with valuable data that could be used to optimize maintenance schedules and improve service delivery.

In industrial settings, the application of Zero Trust to IoT security is equally transformative. Manufacturing plants and industrial control systems (ICS) are increasingly interconnected with IoT devices that monitor everything from equipment performance to environmental conditions. These devices are essential for maintaining operational efficiency, yet they also present significant security risks. A notable case involved an automotive manufacturer that deployed hundreds of IoT sensors throughout its assembly lines to track production metrics in real time. Recognizing the potential for these devices to be exploited by cybercriminals, the manufacturer implemented a Zero Trust framework that isolated IoT devices into their own micro-segments. Each sensor was continuously authenticated, and its data was scrutinized for any signs of abnormal activity. When one sensor began reporting erratic readings—potentially indicative of tampering or malfunction— the system automatically isolated it from the rest of the network and alerted the maintenance team. The rapid response not only prevented a potential production halt but also demonstrated how Zero Trust principles can protect both digital and physical assets. In this context, the convergence of IoT security and Zero Trust not only safeguards the production process but also provides operational intelligence that can lead to improved efficiency and cost savings.

The interplay between remote work and IoT security further complicates the landscape, as many modern organizations rely on a mix of both. A global energy company managing remote field operations might deploy IoT devices at oil rigs and pipelines while also supporting remote offices spread across different time zones. In such scenarios, a Zero Trust approach becomes indispensable. The company might deploy a unified security platform that integrates identity verification, network segmentation, and continuous monitoring across both remote endpoints and IoT devices. This platform would ensure that an engineer accessing data from a remote location undergoes the same rigorous verification process as a sensor transmitting data from a pipeline. In one incident, the unified platform detected an anomalous data pattern from a remote monitoring device at an offshore facility. The system immediately isolated the device and required that any subsequent data transmissions be re-verified through a multi-factor authentication process. This swift action prevented a potential cyberattack that could have disrupted critical energy supplies and underscored the value of a holistic Zero Trust strategy.

Beyond the technical aspects, the increasing volume of data generated by remote work and IoT devices presents challenges in terms of data management and analytics. Advanced analytics and machine learning are critical in parsing through vast amounts of logs, identifying patterns, and flagging anomalies. For instance, a multinational logistics company integrated AI-driven analytics into its security platform to continuously monitor both remote work access patterns and IoT device communications. The system was programmed to establish a baseline of normal behavior—for remote workers, this might include typical login times and access patterns; for IoT devices, regular data transmission intervals and expected performance metrics. When deviations occurred, such as a sudden increase in access attempts from a remote region or a sensor transmitting data at irregular intervals, the system would raise alerts and trigger additional verification protocols. This real-time analysis allowed the company to quickly address potential security breaches and minimize the risk of widespread network infiltration. In practice, such a system not only enhances security but also provides operational insights, enabling proactive maintenance and resource optimization.

Another significant consideration is compliance and regulatory oversight in a landscape defined by remote access and IoT connectivity. Industries such as healthcare, finance, and critical infrastructure are subject to rigorous regulatory standards that mandate strict data protection and continuous monitoring. A global financial institution, for example, utilized its Zero Trust framework to support compliance with regulations like GDPR and PCI DSS. By implementing granular access controls and maintaining comprehensive, real-time logs of every access attempt, the institution was able to demonstrate to regulators that its data protection measures were robust and that any deviations were promptly addressed. This level of transparency not only enhances regulatory compliance but also builds trust with customers and partners who demand the highest levels of data security.

The deployment of Zero Trust in such a multifaceted environment requires organizations to adopt integrated management platforms that consolidate disparate security tools into a unified dashboard. These platforms enable administrators to monitor network activity across remote endpoints, IoT devices, and traditional IT assets from a single interface. For example, a large retail conglomerate implemented an integrated security management solution that provided comprehensive visibility into its sprawling network, encompassing physical stores, cloud-based systems, and remote access points. With this unified approach, security teams could correlate data from various sources, identify emerging threats, and swiftly implement countermeasures. The ability to manage the entire security ecosystem cohesively is a significant advantage in a Zero Trust model, ensuring that no vulnerability goes unnoticed.

Effective governance is also essential when extending Zero Trust principles to remote work and IoT. Traditional security policies, often built around static roles and fixed access rights, must be transformed into dynamic protocols that adjust to real-time risk assessments. This shift requires regular policy reviews and updates, as well as cross-functional collaboration among IT, legal, compliance, and human resources teams. For instance, a technology firm conducted quarterly reviews of its Zero Trust policies, using insights gained from continuous monitoring and incident response data to refine its access controls and authentication protocols. This iterative approach ensures that policies remain relevant and effective in the face of rapidly evolving cyber threats.

Moreover, the success of Zero Trust in a remote and IoT-driven environment is closely linked to the organization's overall culture. Employees must understand that security is a shared responsibility and that every access attempt, whether by a remote worker or an IoT device, is subject to verification. To foster this mindset, many companies have instituted regular training sessions, simulated phishing exercises, and interactive workshops designed to illustrate the importance of robust security practices. For example, a multinational consultancy organized annual security awareness campaigns, featuring real-world scenarios and role-playing exercises that emphasized the critical role of continuous verification in maintaining a secure environment. Such initiatives not only boost compliance with security protocols but also empower employees to become active participants in the organization's defense strategy.

As organizations continue to navigate the complexities of remote work and IoT, the evolution of Zero Trust will undoubtedly accelerate. The rapid pace of technological advancement and the ever-changing nature of cyber threats mean that today's solutions may soon require further refinement. Future innovations—such as quantum-resistant encryption, advanced biometric authentication, and even greater integration of blockchain for secure, immutable logging —promise to further enhance the Zero Trust framework. Organizations must therefore remain agile, continuously reassessing and updating their security measures to stay ahead of emerging threats.

In conclusion, the challenges presented by remote work and IoT demand a security model that is both dynamic and resilient. Zero Trust offers a powerful framework for addressing these challenges by enforcing continuous verification, granular access control, and real-time monitoring across all endpoints, regardless of location or device type. The examples discussed —from multinational consulting firms and global financial institutions to smart cities and industrial manufacturing—demonstrate that when Zero Trust principles are effectively applied, they not only protect critical data and infrastructure but also enhance operational efficiency and regulatory compliance. As remote work becomes increasingly prevalent and IoT devices proliferate, the ability to adapt security measures to this new digital landscape will be paramount. Organizations that embrace Zero Trust will be better equipped to safeguard their assets, maintain business continuity, and foster a culture of security in an era defined by constant change and innovation.

CHAPTER 8: THE FUTURE OF ZERO TRUST

As we look to the horizon of cybersecurity, the evolution of Zero Trust is poised to redefine not only how organizations secure their digital assets but also how they adapt to an ever-changing threat landscape. The future of Zero Trust is a story of continuous innovation, where emerging technologies, evolving risk factors, and shifting business priorities converge to create a security framework that is as dynamic as the world it seeks to protect. In this chapter, we explore the future trajectory of Zero Trust, examining emerging trends, anticipating future challenges, and envisioning how organizations can remain agile and resilient in a digital era defined by rapid change and uncertainty.

The digital world is in a constant state of flux. New technologies emerge, cybercriminals develop more sophisticated tactics, and the boundaries between physical and digital spaces blur further with each passing year. In this context, the traditional perimeter-based security model has long been rendered obsolete, and Zero Trust has emerged as the next logical step in the evolution of cybersecurity. At its core, Zero Trust is built on the simple yet profound premise that trust must be continuously earned and never assumed. Yet, as the complexity of digital ecosystems grows, so too must the sophistication of the Zero Trust framework. The future of this model will likely be defined by an increased reliance on automation, artificial intelligence, and machine learning, as well as by a more holistic integration of diverse security functions into a unified strategy.

One of the most significant drivers of future innovation in Zero Trust is the rapid development of artificial intelligence and machine learning. Today's security systems already leverage

AI to analyze vast amounts of data in real time, detecting anomalies and identifying potential threats with remarkable speed. However, as these technologies mature, they will become even more adept at understanding context, predicting potential attack vectors, and autonomously adapting to new threats. Imagine a future where every access request is evaluated not only against a set of static policies but also against an evolving, AI-generated risk model that adapts to the behavior of users, devices, and even entire networks. In such a scenario, the Zero Trust framework would be capable of learning from each incident, adjusting its parameters in real time to thwart novel attack strategies before they can inflict harm. This level of dynamic adaptability could transform cybersecurity from a reactive discipline into a proactive force that anticipates threats and neutralizes them at the moment of emergence.

The integration of AI-driven analytics with Zero Trust also promises to enhance the precision of threat detection and response. Currently, one of the challenges in cybersecurity is the overwhelming volume of data generated by modern networks and devices, which can lead to alert fatigue and delayed responses. In the future, advanced machine learning algorithms will be able to sift through this data more efficiently, pinpointing subtle indicators of compromise that might otherwise go unnoticed. For example, by analyzing the nuances of network traffic and user behavior over time, an AI system could identify the faintest signals of a coordinated cyberattack, even if those signals are spread across multiple endpoints and geographical locations. This proactive identification of potential breaches would allow organizations to implement countermeasures before a full-scale attack unfolds, significantly reducing both the cost and impact of cyber incidents.

Another key area where the future of Zero Trust will make its mark is in the realm of quantum computing. As quantum computers become more powerful and accessible, they will undoubtedly disrupt many of the cryptographic techniques that underpin current security systems. Traditional encryption methods, which rely on the computational difficulty of certain mathematical problems, may eventually be rendered obsolete by quantum algorithms capable of solving these problems in a fraction of the time. In anticipation of this threat, researchers and industry leaders are already exploring quantum-resistant encryption techniques. In the context of Zero Trust, quantum-safe cryptography will be an essential component of a future-proof security framework. Organizations will need to transition to encryption standards that are resilient to quantum attacks, ensuring that every piece of data—whether at rest or in transit —is protected against the next generation of computational power. The adoption of quantum-resistant technologies will be a major milestone in the evolution of Zero Trust, helping to secure digital environments against threats that, until recently, were only theoretical.

The rise of blockchain technology also holds promise for the future of Zero Trust. Blockchain, with its decentralized and immutable ledger, offers a new paradigm for establishing trust in digital transactions. In a future Zero Trust environment, blockchain could be used to create tamper-proof logs of every access request, transaction, and interaction within an organization's network. Such an immutable record would not only provide unparalleled transparency and accountability but also make it significantly more difficult for attackers to cover their tracks or alter evidence of a breach. For instance, an organization might implement a blockchain-based identity management system where every authentication event is recorded in a decentralized ledger. This would enable security teams to trace any unauthorized access back to its source with certainty, streamlining forensic investigations and improving the overall resilience of the network. As blockchain technology continues to mature, its integration into Zero Trust architectures could redefine how trust and verification are managed across digital ecosystems.

The future of Zero Trust is also inextricably linked with the continued expansion of the Internet of Things. The proliferation of IoT devices has already dramatically increased the number of endpoints within a network, and this trend is set to continue as smart devices become more ubiquitous in homes, cities, and industrial environments. Each IoT device represents a potential entry point for cyberattacks, and the challenge of securing these devices is compounded by their often limited computing resources and inconsistent security standards. Looking ahead, we can expect to see the development of lightweight, IoT-specific security protocols that are designed to integrate seamlessly with Zero Trust architectures. These protocols will likely include advanced methods for continuous device authentication, real-time monitoring, and automated threat response tailored to the unique constraints of IoT hardware. In industrial settings, for example, smart factories and connected supply chains will rely on Zero Trust frameworks to ensure that every sensor, actuator, and controller is continuously verified and isolated from potential threats. This will not only safeguard production processes but also enable the real-time analytics necessary for optimizing operations and reducing downtime.

As remote work continues to redefine the traditional workplace, the future of Zero Trust will also be shaped by the evolving needs of a distributed workforce. The COVID-19 pandemic accelerated the transition to remote work, and it is clear that many organizations are unlikely to return to the old office-centric model. Instead, the modern enterprise will be characterized by a hybrid work environment, where employees operate from a variety of locations using a diverse array of devices. This shift demands a Zero Trust model that is flexible and scalable, capable of securing not just a static network perimeter but a dynamic, constantly shifting landscape of access points. Future Zero Trust solutions will need to incorporate more sophisticated contextual data, including biometric indicators, real-time device diagnostics, and even behavioral analytics that capture the subtle nuances of how an employee interacts with digital systems. For example, a future remote worker might authenticate using a combination of facial recognition, keystroke dynamics, and location-based data, creating a multi-layered verification process that adapts to changes in behavior over time. This adaptive model would ensure that every access request is evaluated against a rich set of data points, reducing the likelihood of unauthorized access even in the most distributed environments.

The transformation of the workplace is not only changing how organizations secure their networks but also how they manage and analyze data. With remote work, the volume of data generated by cloud services, mobile devices, and collaborative platforms is exploding. In the future, Zero Trust will likely be integrated with advanced data analytics platforms that can process this vast amount of information in real time, identifying trends, predicting potential vulnerabilities, and informing strategic decision-making. Such platforms will leverage big data technologies, advanced machine learning algorithms, and even natural language processing to transform raw data into actionable insights. For instance, by analyzing patterns in employee access logs, an organization might identify a gradual shift in behavior that suggests a potential insider threat. Alternatively, by correlating data from various sources, including IoT sensors, network traffic, and user activity, security teams could proactively detect coordinated attacks before they have a chance to escalate. This data-driven approach to Zero Trust not only enhances security but also provides valuable insights that can drive innovation and operational efficiency.

Regulatory and compliance pressures will continue to shape the evolution of Zero Trust in the coming years. As governments around the world enact stricter data protection laws and cybersecurity standards, organizations will be required to adopt more robust security measures to avoid significant penalties and reputational damage. The future of Zero Trust will be closely aligned with these regulatory developments, as compliance becomes a key driver of security innovation. In industries such as finance, healthcare, and critical infrastructure, organizations will need to demonstrate that they are continuously verifying every access attempt and maintaining comprehensive, auditable records of all security events. Future Zero Trust solutions will likely incorporate advanced compliance management tools that automatically generate reports, monitor adherence to regulatory standards, and alert administrators to potential compliance gaps. This integration will not only simplify the process of regulatory reporting but also enhance overall security by ensuring that every aspect of the network is subject to rigorous, ongoing scrutiny.

The evolution of Zero Trust will also be influenced by broader trends in the technology landscape, such as the rise of edge computing. As more data is processed at the edge of the network—closer to where it is generated—the need for distributed security solutions becomes more pressing. In the future, Zero Trust frameworks will extend their reach beyond centralized data centers to encompass a myriad of edge devices and local processing nodes. This will require a rethinking of traditional security architectures, shifting from a centralized model to a more decentralized approach that can secure data and applications at the point of generation. For example, in a smart manufacturing facility, edge computing devices might process real-time production data locally, while still being integrated into the broader Zero Trust framework that verifies and monitors every transaction. This decentralized model will not only reduce latency and improve operational efficiency but also enhance security by minimizing the amount of sensitive data that must be transmitted across potentially vulnerable networks.

Collaboration and integration among different security technologies and vendors will be another critical factor in the future of Zero Trust. As the security landscape becomes more complex, no single solution can address every threat or vulnerability. The future will likely see the emergence of more integrated, interoperable security ecosystems in which diverse tools—from identity management systems and network segmentation solutions to AI-driven analytics platforms and blockchain-based logging systems—work together seamlessly. This integration will be facilitated by standardized protocols, robust APIs, and industry-wide collaboration, ensuring that organizations can build a cohesive security posture without being locked into proprietary systems. Such interoperability will empower security teams to leverage the best available technologies and quickly adapt to emerging threats, thereby enhancing both the effectiveness and the resilience of the Zero Trust model.

Furthermore, the cultural and organizational shifts that have already begun in response to Zero Trust will continue to evolve. In the future, the principles of Zero Trust will be embedded not only in technical systems but also in the very fabric of organizational culture. Security will be viewed as a shared responsibility, with every employee, from the C-suite to front-line workers, playing an active role in maintaining a secure environment. This cultural transformation will be driven by ongoing education, transparent communication, and a commitment to continuous improvement. Organizations that embrace this mindset will be better prepared to adapt to the dynamic challenges of cybersecurity, ensuring that their defenses remain robust even as the threat landscape evolves.

Looking further ahead, the convergence of Zero Trust with emerging paradigms such as digital twins and augmented reality may further transform cybersecurity. Digital twins—virtual replicas of physical systems—are already being used to simulate and optimize industrial processes. In the future, digital twins could serve as testbeds for security scenarios, allowing organizations to model the impact of cyberattacks and refine their Zero Trust strategies in a controlled environment.

Similarly, augmented reality (AR) could be employed to provide real-time visualizations of network activity and threat intelligence, enabling security teams to "see" potential vulnerabilities and respond more quickly to emerging issues. These futuristic applications may seem like science fiction today, but they represent the next frontier in a continuous effort to stay ahead of cyber adversaries.

In summary, the future of Zero Trust is a dynamic tapestry woven from threads of technological innovation, evolving threat landscapes, regulatory imperatives, and cultural transformation. As organizations look ahead, they must embrace a security framework that is as agile and adaptive as the digital environments in which they operate. Continuous verification, real-time analytics, quantum-resistant encryption, blockchain-based logging, and the integration of edge computing will all play pivotal roles in shaping the next generation of Zero Trust. The ability to learn from every interaction, adjust security protocols on the fly, and maintain a rigorous, distributed defense will be essential for thriving in a world where the only constant is change.

Ultimately, the evolution of Zero Trust is not a destination but a journey—one that requires relentless innovation, interdisciplinary collaboration, and a commitment to perpetual improvement. Organizations that invest in the future of Zero Trust will not only fortify their digital ecosystems against tomorrow's threats but will also create a competitive advantage in an increasingly interconnected world. By continuously rethinking what it means to trust and by leveraging the latest technological advancements, these organizations will transform security from a reactive necessity into a proactive, strategic asset. In this brave new world, trust is not granted by default; it is earned, measured, and continuously reinforced through rigorous, real-time verification.

As we look forward, the promise of Zero Trust is both exciting and daunting. The challenges ahead are significant, yet the potential rewards—a more secure, resilient, and innovative digital landscape—are immense. The journey toward a truly Zero Trust future will require organizations to remain vigilant, adaptive, and forward-thinking. They must be prepared to embrace change, invest in cutting-edge technologies, and cultivate a culture of security that permeates every aspect of their operations. In doing so, they will not only protect their critical assets but also pave the way for a new era of trust, where every connection is secure, every transaction is verified, and every digital interaction contributes to a safer, more resilient world.

In conclusion, the future of Zero Trust is a compelling vision of a digital ecosystem where security is continuously verified, dynamically managed, and inherently adaptive. As remote work, IoT, edge computing, quantum technologies, and blockchain converge, the evolution of Zero Trust will shape the next generation of cybersecurity. It is a future where organizations are empowered to respond to threats in real time, where the integrity of every access request is upheld, and where trust is not a given but a continuously earned asset. For those willing to invest in this transformative journey, the rewards will be profound—a secure, agile, and future-proof digital world that stands resilient in the face of ever-evolving challenges.

CHAPTER 9: ZERO TRUST AND DEVSECOPS INTEGRATION

The digital transformation of organizations has not only reshaped traditional IT operations but also revolutionized the way software is developed, deployed, and maintained. In this landscape, Zero Trust and DevSecOps integration has emerged as a vital convergence of security, development, and operations, where the objective is to ensure that every element of the software delivery process is secure by design. This chapter explores in depth how Zero Trust principles can be seamlessly woven into the DevSecOps culture and practices, transforming the way organizations build and maintain secure applications in an era defined by rapid change and continuous innovation.

The evolution of IT over the past decade has seen a dramatic shift from siloed security practices to a more integrated, continuous approach. Traditionally, security teams operated separately from development and operations, with a heavy reliance on periodic reviews, manual testing, and end-of-cycle audits. However, with the rise of agile methodologies and continuous integration and delivery pipelines, this separation has become a critical vulnerability. In a modern DevSecOps environment, security must be embedded into every stage of the software development lifecycle, from initial planning and design through to coding, testing, deployment, and maintenance. Zero Trust plays a central role in this transformation by providing a framework that assumes no component, process, or interaction is inherently trustworthy.

Integrating Zero Trust into DevSecOps begins with a fundamental shift in mindset. Rather than treating security as a separate phase to be tacked on at the end of the development cycle, organizations adopting Zero Trust view it as an integral component that informs every decision and process. In practical terms, this means that every code commit, every build, and every deployment is subject to continuous verification. For instance, imagine a scenario in which a developer submits code to a shared repository. In a Zero Trust-enabled DevSecOps pipeline, that code is automatically scanned for vulnerabilities, its dependencies are verified against known safe libraries, and its execution context is evaluated before it can be merged into the main branch. This level of scrutiny ensures that even if a vulnerability is inadvertently introduced, it is caught and remediated before it has the opportunity to be exploited in production environments.

Automation is one of the key drivers that enable this level of continuous security. Modern DevSecOps pipelines are replete with automated tools and processes that ensure every component of an application is validated against security policies in real time. Automated static and dynamic analysis tools scan source code and running applications for known vulnerabilities, while continuous integration systems run a battery of tests to ensure that every change meets stringent quality and security standards. In the context of Zero Trust, automation goes further by incorporating risk-based verification into each step. For example, if a component of the application exhibits behavior that deviates from its expected baseline, automated systems can immediately trigger additional security checks, enforce stricter access controls, or even roll back the deployment until the issue is resolved. This tight feedback loop not only accelerates the remediation process but also reduces the window of opportunity for potential attackers to exploit vulnerabilities.

One illustrative example of this integration can be seen in the experience of a global financial institution that modernized its software delivery process. In the past, the institution relied on periodic security audits and manual penetration testing to secure its applications. However, as the volume of code and the speed of deployments increased, these measures became inadequate. By integrating Zero Trust principles into its DevSecOps pipeline, the institution reengineered its processes so that every new code deployment was automatically subjected to rigorous security verification. When a vulnerability was detected during the automated scanning phase, the system immediately flagged it, and the developer was required to address the issue before the code could progress further. Over time, this approach significantly reduced the number of vulnerabilities in production and led to a culture in which developers themselves became more security-aware, routinely writing code with built-in security controls and constantly monitoring for anomalies. The success of this integration was not measured solely by the reduction in breaches but also by the overall agility and resilience of the development process, which allowed the institution to respond rapidly to emerging threats while maintaining regulatory compliance.

Another dimension of integrating Zero Trust with DevSecOps is the role of continuous monitoring and real-time analytics. Traditional security practices often involved periodic reviews and static threat models that were quickly rendered obsolete by the pace of modern cyber threats. In a Zero Trust DevSecOps environment, continuous monitoring provides a live feed of information that is used to validate every interaction within the system. This includes not only the activity of users and applications but also the behavior of infrastructure components such as containers, virtual machines, and serverless functions. For instance, a cloud-native application may be deployed across a distributed microservices architecture, where each service communicates over APIs. By implementing continuous monitoring, an organization can track these API calls in real time, identify unusual patterns or deviations from expected performance, and trigger automated responses if anomalies are detected. This level of granular visibility is essential for maintaining the integrity of a Zero Trust environment, as it ensures that every component is continuously validated and that any deviation from the norm is immediately addressed.

Integrating Zero Trust into DevSecOps also requires a rethinking of identity and access management. In a traditional setting, developers and operators often had broad access privileges that allowed them to make changes directly to production environments. However, this "trust by default" approach is antithetical to the principles of Zero Trust. Instead, organizations must enforce the principle of least privilege throughout the DevSecOps pipeline, ensuring that every user, process, and device is granted only the minimum level of access necessary to perform its function. For example, a software development team might implement role-based access control (RBAC) policies that restrict access to production systems, such that even senior developers cannot deploy changes without undergoing additional verification steps. This might involve multi-factor authentication, just-in-time access provisioning, or even biometric verification in high-risk scenarios. The goal is to minimize the attack surface by ensuring that every access request is scrutinized and that no user or system is given free rein without proving its legitimacy.

One of the challenges in integrating Zero Trust with DevSecOps is balancing the need for security with the need for speed and agility. In today's fast-paced digital environment, organizations cannot afford to slow down development cycles by imposing cumbersome security processes. Therefore, the integration must be designed in a way that security checks are as seamless and automated as possible. This is where the convergence of continuous integration/continuous deployment (CI/CD) tools with security automation becomes critical. Modern CI/CD pipelines can incorporate security tests as part of the build process, ensuring that any code that fails to meet security criteria is automatically rejected. Moreover, these pipelines can be configured to dynamically adjust security policies based on contextual risk assessments. For instance, if an application is being deployed during off-peak hours or from a less secure network environment, the system might automatically enforce additional layers of authentication or limit certain functionalities until further checks are completed. This dynamic adjustment ensures that the pace of development is not compromised while still maintaining a robust security posture.

The cultural transformation required for successful Zero Trust and DevSecOps integration cannot be overstated. It demands that every member of the organization, from executive leadership to individual developers, internalizes the idea that security is a shared responsibility. This cultural shift is often achieved through continuous education, training programs, and regular communication about security best practices. Organizations that have successfully integrated these principles often hold regular "security huddles" or collaborative workshops where teams discuss recent incidents, share lessons learned, and update their processes accordingly. In one case study, a multinational technology company introduced a "shift-left" approach, encouraging developers to incorporate security considerations from the very beginning of the design phase. This approach not only led to a significant reduction in vulnerabilities but also fostered a sense of ownership among developers, who began to see security as an integral part of their craft rather than an external imposition. The result was a more agile, resilient, and secure software delivery process that could rapidly adapt to emerging threats.

Another important aspect of this integration is the role of collaboration between development, security, and operations teams. In many traditional organizations, these groups operated in silos, each with its own set of priorities and workflows. However, the rapid evolution of cyber threats has made it clear that a coordinated approach is essential. By integrating Zero Trust into DevSecOps, organizations can create cross-functional teams that work together from the earliest stages of the software lifecycle. These teams share tools, data, and insights, enabling them to identify and mitigate risks more effectively. For example, a financial services company might establish a dedicated security operations center (SOC) that collaborates closely with development teams to monitor application behavior, analyze potential vulnerabilities, and implement rapid remediation measures. This collaborative approach not only enhances security but also drives innovation, as teams learn from each other and continuously refine their processes in response to real-world challenges.

The integration of emerging technologies further enhances the synergy between Zero Trust and DevSecOps. As artificial intelligence and machine learning algorithms become more sophisticated, they are being deployed to automate and optimize security processes. These technologies can analyze vast amounts of data generated by CI/CD pipelines, user interactions, and network traffic, providing real-time insights that inform security policies. For instance, an AI-driven security system might identify subtle anomalies in code commits or detect patterns of behavior that suggest a potential insider threat. By automatically flagging these issues for further investigation, the system reduces the burden on human analysts and speeds up the overall response time. This proactive approach is particularly valuable in a DevSecOps environment, where the rapid pace of development demands that security controls be both effective and efficient.

As organizations continue to evolve their DevSecOps practices under the Zero Trust model, the importance of compliance and regulatory oversight becomes increasingly apparent. Many industries, such as healthcare, finance, and government, operate under strict regulatory frameworks that demand robust data protection and continuous monitoring. Zero Trust offers a powerful way to meet these regulatory requirements by providing detailed, real-time logs of every access attempt and transaction within the software delivery process. These logs not only serve as a valuable resource for incident response and forensic investigations but also help demonstrate compliance during audits. For example, a healthcare organization might use its Zero Trust-enabled DevSecOps pipeline to generate comprehensive reports that document every instance of access to patient data, ensuring that they can provide evidence of compliance with regulations like HIPAA. Such transparency not only mitigates regulatory risk but also builds trust with customers and partners who are increasingly concerned about data security.

Looking to the future, the integration of Zero Trust and DevSecOps is likely to continue evolving, driven by both technological advances and shifting organizational needs. One emerging trend is the increasing use of containerization and orchestration platforms, such as Kubernetes, to deploy applications in cloud environments. These platforms introduce new security challenges, as containerized applications can be highly ephemeral and dynamic. However, they also provide new opportunities for implementing Zero Trust controls at a granular level. For instance, each container can be isolated in its own micro-segment, with strict access controls and continuous monitoring applied to every process within the container. This not only limits the potential impact of a breach but also allows organizations to scale their security practices dynamically as applications are deployed and decommissioned. As containerization becomes more prevalent, we can expect to see further innovations in security tools that are specifically designed to work within these environments, integrating seamlessly with existing CI/CD pipelines and DevSecOps processes.

Another frontier for Zero Trust and DevSecOps integration is the increasing emphasis on supply chain security. In today's interconnected world, software supply chains have become a prime target for attackers, as vulnerabilities in third-party components can compromise entire applications. The recent surge in supply chain attacks has underscored the need for a Zero Trust approach that extends beyond the boundaries of the organization's own codebase. By incorporating automated scanning and verification of third-party libraries and dependencies into the DevSecOps pipeline, organizations can detect and mitigate vulnerabilities before they become exploitable. This proactive stance on supply chain security not only reduces risk but also encourages a culture of transparency and collaboration among vendors and partners, ultimately contributing to a more secure overall ecosystem.

In practical terms, the integration of Zero Trust with DevSecOps is a journey rather than a destination. It requires continuous iteration, feedback, and improvement, as well as a willingness to embrace change at both the technological and cultural levels. Organizations that have successfully navigated this journey have often started with pilot projects or proof-of-concept initiatives, gradually expanding their scope as they gain confidence in the new model. They invest in advanced automation, leverage real-time analytics, and foster cross-functional collaboration to create a resilient security framework that evolves with the threat landscape. Over time, this integrated approach not only reduces vulnerabilities but also accelerates the development process, as security becomes an enabler of innovation rather than an obstacle to rapid delivery.

In conclusion, Zero Trust and DevSecOps integration represents a fundamental shift in how organizations approach software development, security, and operations. By embedding continuous verification, automated risk assessment, and granular access controls into every stage of the software delivery lifecycle, organizations can build systems that are inherently secure, agile, and resilient. The transformation requires a cultural shift, robust collaboration among cross-functional teams, and the adoption of emerging technologies that automate and optimize security processes. As organizations embrace this new paradigm, they not only protect their digital assets from increasingly sophisticated threats but also position themselves to innovate more rapidly in an ever-changing digital landscape.

The journey toward a fully integrated Zero Trust DevSecOps model is both challenging and rewarding. It calls for a rethinking of established practices and a commitment to continuous improvement, where every interaction is an opportunity to verify, validate, and secure the environment. For organizations willing to invest in this transformation, the benefits extend far beyond reduced risk—they include improved agility, greater operational efficiency, and a stronger competitive position in a market where security and speed are equally valued.

As we look to the future, the convergence of Zero Trust and DevSecOps will continue to shape the evolution of cybersecurity. With each new technological breakthrough and every lesson learned from real-world applications, the framework becomes more refined, more adaptive, and more deeply embedded in the fabric of modern IT. In this brave new world, trust is not granted by default but is earned through a relentless commitment to continuous verification and improvement. For organizations that embrace this paradigm, the promise of a secure, agile, and innovative digital future is well within reach.

CHAPTER 10: ZERO TRUST FOR SMALL AND MEDIUM ENTERPRISES (SMES)

Small and medium enterprises (SMEs) are often compared to nimble speedboats that navigate rapidly changing waters, while large corporations are more like massive ships with complex systems and long-established procedures. For SMEs, every dollar counts, and every decision can have an outsized impact on the company's survival. In the realm of cybersecurity, this means that SMEs must balance the need for robust protection against the reality of limited budgets, fewer dedicated IT security personnel, and rapidly evolving threats. Zero Trust offers an especially appealing framework for SMEs because its fundamental principle—that no user, device, or application is inherently trustworthy—can be scaled to fit any organization, regardless of size. In this chapter, we explore how SMEs can adopt Zero Trust principles, discuss the unique challenges and opportunities they face, and examine real-world examples and analogies that shed light on how a Zero Trust approach can be both cost-effective and transformative.

Imagine a small business like a neighborhood bakery that has grown steadily over the years. Initially, the bakery relied on a simple cash register and a basic accounting system. As the business expanded, it started to adopt digital systems for inventory management, customer orders, and employee scheduling. With this digital transformation came new challenges—online orders, payment processing, and sensitive customer data all needed protection. In this context, the bakery's management began to realize that traditional "trusted" systems, which assumed that employees working behind a secure door could be trusted, were no longer sufficient. Just as the bakery might install multiple locks and alarms to safeguard its premises, SMEs must adopt multiple layers of security to protect their digital assets. Zero Trust, with its "never trust, always verify" approach, offers a blueprint for building these layers systematically.

For many SMEs, one of the primary challenges is limited financial and human resources. Unlike large corporations that can allocate millions of dollars to cybersecurity, SMEs must be strategic in their investments. However, the beauty of Zero Trust lies in its flexibility. It does not require a complete overhaul of existing systems overnight but can be implemented incrementally. Consider an analogy: upgrading a modest home's security does not mean replacing every lock and installing a full-scale surveillance system immediately. Instead, the homeowner might start by installing a smart lock on the front door, adding motion sensors in critical areas, and gradually integrating a video doorbell that links to a mobile app. Over time, these incremental improvements build into a comprehensive security system. Similarly, SMEs can begin their Zero Trust journey by identifying critical assets—such as customer databases, financial records, or intellectual property—and focusing on protecting those first. This phased approach allows them to allocate resources wisely and build confidence in the system as they progress.

One effective starting point for SMEs is to conduct a thorough assessment of their current IT landscape. This means mapping out every device, user, and application that accesses the company's network. It's akin to a small business owner taking inventory of all the keys and locks in a house before deciding which ones to upgrade. In many cases, SMEs discover that they have "shadow IT" systems—applications or devices that have been added ad hoc without proper oversight—which represent significant vulnerabilities. By gaining visibility into these assets, the business can begin to apply Zero Trust principles, ensuring that every device and user is authenticated and that access is granted strictly on a need-to-know basis.

One real-world example comes from a regional accounting firm that, until recently, had relied on a traditional firewall-based security model. As the firm expanded and more employees began working remotely, management noticed a rise in phishing attacks and unauthorized access attempts. With limited resources and a small IT team, the firm could not afford to invest in expensive, enterprise-level security systems. Instead, they adopted a Zero Trust approach by leveraging cloud-based identity and access management (IAM) solutions that offered continuous multi-factor authentication. Every time an accountant logged into the firm's cloud-based accounting software, they were prompted to verify their identity using a combination of passwords, SMS-based codes, and, in some cases, biometric scans from their smartphones. The system also monitored unusual behavior such as logins from foreign IP addresses or during odd hours, automatically flagging or even blocking suspicious access. Within six months, the firm reported a significant reduction in security incidents and gained a greater sense of control over their digital environment—all while staying within a tight budget.

Another important factor for SMEs is the scalability of security solutions. Many large-scale security platforms are designed with the assumption that they will serve thousands of users and devices. For an SME, however, such solutions can be overly complex and expensive. Zero Trust for SMEs, therefore, emphasizes cost-effective strategies that scale with the organization. Cloud-based security services offer pay-as-you-go models, allowing small businesses to access enterprise-grade protection without a massive upfront investment. For instance, a local retail chain with five stores might use a cloud-based Zero Trust platform to manage employee access to point-of-sale systems, inventory databases, and customer relationship management tools. By integrating continuous monitoring and risk-based access controls, the system ensures that each employee only accesses the information they need. This not only reduces the risk of internal breaches but also streamlines operations—much like a well-organized store where every employee has a specific role and access to only the necessary areas of the store, reducing the risk of theft or loss.

Beyond the technical implementations, a crucial element of Zero Trust for SMEs is building a culture of security awareness. In many smaller organizations, security has traditionally been viewed as a technical issue relegated to the IT department. However, in the Zero Trust model, every employee becomes a stakeholder in the organization's cybersecurity posture. Consider the analogy of a small community where everyone looks out for one another. If one neighbor notices suspicious activity, they alert the community, and together, they ensure that everyone remains safe. In a similar vein, SMEs can foster an environment where every employee is educated on the importance of cybersecurity practices such as recognizing phishing emails, using strong, unique passwords, and understanding the reasons behind multi-factor authentication. Regular training sessions, simulated cyberattacks, and clear communication of security policies empower employees to become active participants in the defense strategy. Over time, this culture of security not only reduces the likelihood of human error but also builds a resilient organization where trust is continually verified.

One challenge that many SMEs face is the integration of legacy systems into a modern Zero Trust framework. Often, small businesses have been using the same software and hardware for years—systems that were never designed with modern cybersecurity threats in mind. Upgrading these systems can be costly and disruptive, so SMEs must find ways to bridge the old with the new. One approach is to deploy intermediary solutions such as virtual private networks (VPNs) and secure gateways that can add layers of protection around legacy applications. Think of it like retrofitting an older building with modern alarm systems and reinforced doors; while the building's structure remains the same, its vulnerability to break-ins is significantly reduced. In one illustrative case, a manufacturing SME with decades-old production management software integrated a Zero Trust layer by using a secure API gateway. This gateway intercepted every access attempt, authenticated the request, and ensured that only authorized data transactions occurred. This not only extended the life of the legacy system but also provided enhanced security without the need for a complete overhaul.

Cost-effectiveness is another major concern for SMEs. Implementing a comprehensive Zero Trust model might seem like a luxury reserved for large corporations, but in reality, many Zero Trust solutions are designed to be modular and scalable. SMEs can start small and gradually expand their security posture as the business grows. Cloud services, for instance, offer flexible pricing models that allow companies to pay only for what they use. For example, an e-commerce startup may initially deploy a cloud-based Zero Trust IAM solution to secure its website and customer database. As the company expands, additional modules such as endpoint detection and response (EDR) and continuous monitoring tools can be added incrementally. This pay-as-you-grow model ensures that security investments remain aligned with the business's revenue and growth trajectory, much like a small business owner who reinvests profits gradually to upgrade equipment or expand the shop.

SMEs also benefit from the agility that Zero Trust provides. In today's fast-paced business environment, the ability to quickly adapt to new threats is crucial. Traditional security models often involve lengthy procurement cycles and rigid policies that cannot keep pace with the rapid evolution of cyber threats. Zero Trust, with its continuous verification and dynamic risk assessment, allows SMEs to respond to incidents in real time. For instance, if a small marketing firm detects unusual access patterns on its cloud-based client database, the Zero Trust system can automatically adjust access controls, temporarily restrict access, and alert the IT team—all within minutes. This rapid response capability minimizes the damage from potential breaches and ensures that critical business operations can continue with minimal disruption.

Analogies can be particularly useful in understanding the benefits of Zero Trust for SMEs. Consider a small family-owned restaurant. In the past, the restaurant might have relied on a single, large safe to store all its cash, assuming that once the door was locked at night, the money was secure. However, if a burglar managed to crack the safe, all the cash would be lost. With a Zero Trust approach, the restaurant would instead distribute its cash across several smaller safes in different locations. Even if one safe were compromised, only a fraction of the total funds would be at risk. Similarly, by implementing granular access controls and segmenting their networks, SMEs can ensure that even if one part of the system is breached, the overall damage is contained. This compartmentalization not only reduces risk but also simplifies the process of identifying and addressing vulnerabilities.

Real-world case studies further illustrate how Zero Trust can be successfully implemented in SME environments. Take, for instance, a regional logistics company with a fleet of delivery vehicles and a central dispatch system. Previously, the company relied on a single firewall and basic antivirus software to protect its systems. However, as the company expanded and more vehicles were equipped with digital tracking systems, the security risks multiplied. Cybercriminals began targeting the tracking devices to manipulate delivery routes and steal sensitive customer information. Recognizing the escalating threat, the company adopted a Zero Trust model that included continuous device authentication, network segmentation, and real-time monitoring of data transmissions. Every vehicle was assigned a unique digital identity, and its communication with the central system was continuously verified. If a vehicle's tracking device behaved abnormally—such as transmitting data from an unexpected location—the system would isolate the device and alert security personnel. This proactive strategy not only thwarted several attempted breaches but also improved operational efficiency by providing detailed analytics on fleet performance and route optimization. The logistics company's experience highlights that, for SMEs, Zero Trust is not merely a defensive measure but a strategic tool that can drive business improvements and operational insights.

Another compelling example comes from a small software-as-a-service (SaaS) company that provides online project management tools to local businesses. With a small team of developers and limited IT resources, the company initially struggled to balance the need for rapid feature development with the imperative of robust security. After a minor data breach that exposed customer project details, the company re-evaluated its security posture and decided to adopt a Zero Trust framework. They implemented a cloud-based identity management system that required continuous multi-factor authentication and integrated automated vulnerability scanning into their continuous integration/continuous deployment (CI/CD) pipeline. Developers were trained to adopt "security-first" coding practices, and every change was automatically tested against a set of predefined security benchmarks. Over the next year, not only did the company see a dramatic reduction in security incidents, but the improved security measures also instilled greater confidence among its clients, leading to increased customer retention and positive word-of-mouth. This example underscores the dual benefits of Zero Trust for SMEs: enhanced security and improved business performance.

Zero Trust for SMEs also means rethinking the approach to vendor management and third-party integrations. Many small businesses rely on external service providers for functions such as payroll, customer relationship management, and even cybersecurity. Each of these third-party connections represents a potential vulnerability if not managed properly. By applying Zero Trust principles, SMEs can ensure that every external interaction is scrutinized. For example, a local retail chain might integrate its payment processing system with a third-party vendor, but only after ensuring that the vendor adheres to the same strict access controls and continuous monitoring protocols as the internal systems. The retail chain could implement a secure API gateway that verifies each transaction between its systems and the vendor's services, reducing the risk of a breach originating from an external source. In this way, Zero Trust extends beyond the confines of the organization, creating a secure ecosystem in which all partners and suppliers are held to the same high standards.

In addition to technical and operational strategies, the success of Zero Trust in an SME environment hinges on leadership and governance. SME owners and managers must view cybersecurity not as a cost center but as a critical component of overall business strategy. By allocating resources to security measures that align with Zero Trust principles, they can safeguard their businesses against the rising tide of cyber threats while also enhancing operational efficiency. This shift in mindset is akin to investing in preventive healthcare—spending money now to avoid much larger costs later in the form of data breaches, downtime, or reputational damage. Many SMEs have found that even modest investments in Zero Trust technologies —such as cloud-based IAM solutions, endpoint detection and response systems, and secure VPNs—pay dividends in terms of reduced risk and improved customer confidence.

One of the most compelling aspects of Zero Trust for SMEs is its ability to scale with the organization. As a small business grows, its security needs evolve, and a Zero Trust framework can adapt to these changing requirements. For instance, a startup that begins with a handful of employees and a single office may initially implement basic security measures such as multi-factor authentication and regular vulnerability scans. As the company expands to multiple locations, incorporates remote work, and integrates more complex systems, the Zero Trust framework can evolve to include advanced analytics, network segmentation, and comprehensive monitoring tools. This scalability ensures that security remains robust without requiring a complete overhaul every time the business grows—a critical factor for SMEs that must carefully manage their budgets and resources.

Analogies often help clarify complex concepts, and one useful analogy for Zero Trust in SMEs is that of a medieval castle. In a traditional castle, the outer walls and moats were the primary means of defense, creating a clear distinction between the safe interior and the dangerous outside world. However, once an invader breached the outer defenses, the inner chambers were vulnerable. Zero Trust is like having a castle where every room is locked, and every visitor must be checked at every door, regardless of whether they're coming from the courtyard or the main gate. Even trusted knights and servants must present credentials every time they move from one chamber to another. For an SME, this means that even employees, partners, and systems that are inside the "castle" must continuously prove their legitimacy before accessing critical information or resources. This multi-layered approach ensures that even if one layer of defense is compromised, the overall security of the organization remains intact.

Another analogy can be drawn from the world of personal finance. Consider a person who manages multiple bank accounts, investment portfolios, and credit cards. Rather than keeping all funds in a single account, they diversify their assets across various accounts, each protected by its own set of security measures. They may use two-factor authentication for online banking, set up transaction alerts, and even maintain separate passwords for different accounts. In this way, if one account is compromised, the damage is contained, and the person's overall financial security is not jeopardized. Similarly, an SME that implements Zero Trust divides its digital assets into segmented zones, applies tailored access controls for each, and continuously monitors every interaction. This diversification of security measures ensures that even if one segment is breached, the overall integrity of the organization is maintained.

In conclusion, Zero Trust for small and medium enterprises is not an all-or-nothing proposition; it is a flexible, scalable framework that can be tailored to meet the unique needs and constraints of smaller organizations. By understanding their current security posture, investing in cost-effective, cloud-based solutions, fostering a culture of continuous verification, and leveraging both technical and operational best practices, SMEs can build a robust security foundation that evolves with their business. Whether you are a local bakery, a regional logistics company, or a burgeoning tech startup, the principles of Zero Trust offer a roadmap to a secure digital future—one where every interaction is scrutinized, every asset is protected, and trust is continuously earned.

Through real-world examples and relatable analogies, it becomes clear that the journey to Zero Trust is both challenging and rewarding. SMEs that embark on this journey not only protect themselves from the ever-growing threats of the cyber world but also unlock new opportunities for efficiency, customer trust, and sustainable growth. In a rapidly changing digital environment, the adoption of Zero Trust is not just a defensive measure—it is a strategic investment in the resilience and future success of the organization.

CHAPTER 11: LEGAL, REGULATORY, AND ETHICAL CONSIDERATIONS

In an era where digital transformations are occurring at breakneck speed and cyber threats are evolving every day, organizations must not only invest in robust technical defenses but also navigate a complex web of legal, regulatory, and ethical requirements. As Zero Trust has emerged as a leading security paradigm that demands continuous verification and stringent access controls, it has also introduced a host of challenges in the legal and ethical arenas. This chapter examines how the Zero Trust model intersects with legal mandates, regulatory frameworks, and ethical considerations. By exploring real-world examples, drawing analogies, and discussing evolving policies, we gain a clearer picture of the responsibilities organizations bear in protecting data, preserving privacy, and ensuring fair practices.

To begin with, the essence of Zero Trust—"never trust, always verify"—has profound legal implications. At its core, Zero Trust requires that every access request, whether from an internal employee or an external partner, undergoes rigorous scrutiny. This means that organizations must maintain detailed logs, continuously monitor network activity, and often collect sensitive personal data to verify identities. In many jurisdictions, however, the collection, storage, and use of personal data are strictly regulated by laws such as the European Union's General Data Protection Regulation (GDPR), the Health Insurance Portability and Accountability Act (HIPAA) in the United States, and various other data protection laws around the world. For example, a European-based financial institution implementing Zero Trust might need to reconcile its continuous monitoring practices with GDPR's requirements for data minimization and user consent. The challenge lies in ensuring that the security measures do not inadvertently violate privacy rights or overreach the bounds set by regulatory bodies.

Consider an analogy: think of an organization as a high-security bank. In order to protect the vault, the bank installs cameras and motion detectors throughout its premises. However, these devices must be installed in a way that respects the privacy of employees and customers. If the bank were to record every conversation or track every movement without transparency or legitimate purpose, it would quickly run afoul of privacy laws. Similarly, a Zero Trust environment must strike a balance between comprehensive monitoring for security and respect for individual privacy. Organizations must design systems that not only verify access but also limit the collection of personal data to what is strictly necessary for authentication and risk management. This may involve techniques such as data anonymization or aggregation, where detailed logs are transformed into summary reports that cannot be traced back to specific individuals without additional context.

Legal frameworks are constantly evolving, and as organizations adopt Zero Trust, they must remain agile in adapting to new legislation and regulatory guidance. For instance, the California Consumer Privacy Act (CCPA) has introduced strict requirements on how companies handle personal data, giving consumers rights over the data collected about them. A retail company implementing Zero Trust for its online platform may need to ensure that continuous monitoring systems do not inadvertently capture excessive personal information from customers or employees. In practice, this might require the implementation of data retention policies that automatically purge logs after a certain period or the use of encryption and access controls that restrict who can view detailed records. By integrating compliance into their Zero Trust architectures, organizations can minimize legal exposure while still maintaining the high level of security demanded by the model.

The integration of legal requirements into Zero Trust is not solely a technical exercise; it is also an exercise in governance and organizational policy. Many organizations establish internal compliance teams that work closely with IT and security departments to ensure that all security measures align with applicable laws. This collaborative approach is essential because the legal landscape is inherently dynamic—new regulations emerge, and existing laws are amended in response to technological advances and societal concerns. For example, after a series of high-profile data breaches, lawmakers around the world have been moving to tighten cybersecurity standards. Companies that implement Zero Trust must be prepared to adjust their processes and technologies in response to these changes. Regular audits, both internal and by third-party experts, become a critical part of the Zero Trust lifecycle. These audits not only verify that security controls are effective but also that they remain compliant with legal and regulatory requirements.

A significant legal challenge in the Zero Trust model is ensuring that security measures do not infringe on individual rights. This brings us to the ethical dimension of cybersecurity. Ethical considerations in Zero Trust revolve around questions of privacy, fairness, and accountability. When an organization collects and analyzes vast amounts of data to continuously verify every access attempt, it must consider whether these practices are fair and proportionate. One common ethical concern is the potential for intrusive surveillance. Employees, for instance, may feel uncomfortable knowing that every keystroke, login attempt, or access to a file is being monitored in real time. This constant oversight, if not handled sensitively, could lead to a culture of mistrust or even create an environment where employees feel they have no privacy at work. An analogy can be drawn to the modern workplace in which surveillance cameras monitor every corner of an office building. While such measures can deter theft and misconduct, they can also make employees feel as though they are constantly under scrutiny, potentially stifling creativity and open communication. Organizations must find ways to implement Zero Trust that respect employee dignity and privacy while still achieving the security objectives.

One strategy for addressing ethical concerns is transparency. Organizations should openly communicate their security policies and explain why continuous monitoring is necessary. For instance, a tech startup might hold regular town hall meetings where the IT department explains how Zero Trust measures protect both company assets and personal information. By framing security as a shared responsibility and demonstrating that monitoring is used solely for the purpose of protecting the organization, employees are more likely to see these measures as beneficial rather than punitive. Additionally, organizations can establish ethical guidelines that govern how data is collected, used, and stored. This might include setting strict limits on the duration for which logs are kept, ensuring that data is used only for security purposes, and implementing robust access controls so that only authorized personnel can view sensitive information. These ethical safeguards help to balance the need for security with the imperative to respect individual privacy.

Legal and ethical considerations also extend to how organizations manage relationships with vendors and third-party service providers. In today's interconnected digital ecosystem, many companies rely on external partners for everything from cloud hosting and payment processing to customer relationship management. Each of these partnerships introduces additional layers of complexity from a legal and regulatory standpoint. For example, a small e-commerce company that outsources its IT infrastructure must ensure that its vendors comply with the same strict security standards as the internal systems. This might involve contractual clauses that mandate adherence to specific cybersecurity protocols, regular audits of the vendor's systems, and clear definitions of liability in the event of a breach. The analogy here is similar to hiring a contractor to renovate your home: you need to ensure that the contractor follows building codes and safety standards because any lapse could not only compromise the project but also expose you to legal liability. In the context of Zero Trust, managing vendor relationships becomes a critical aspect of overall risk management, ensuring that the entire supply chain of digital services is secure and compliant with relevant laws.

Another layer of complexity in the legal and ethical dimensions of Zero Trust is the potential for bias and discrimination. When security systems use artificial intelligence and machine learning to analyze user behavior and assign risk scores, there is a risk that these algorithms could inadvertently reinforce existing biases or create new forms of discrimination. For instance, if a risk assessment algorithm is trained on data that predominantly represents one demographic group, it might unfairly flag behavior from users outside that group as anomalous, even if it is perfectly normal for them. This could result in certain employees facing more frequent or stringent verification processes simply due to factors that are not related to their actual security risk. To mitigate such issues, organizations must ensure that their algorithms are transparent, regularly audited for bias, and continually updated to reflect a diverse range of user behaviors. The challenge is analogous to a loan approval system that must evaluate applicants fairly across different socioeconomic backgrounds; just as lending institutions must avoid discriminatory practices in credit scoring, security systems must strive to be impartial and equitable in their risk assessments.

Ethical considerations also arise in the context of data ownership and consent. With Zero Trust, vast amounts of data are generated and stored as part of continuous monitoring and access verification. This data can include sensitive personal information about employees, customers, and partners. Organizations must navigate the fine line between collecting enough data to secure their networks and overstepping into invasive surveillance. In many cases, obtaining explicit consent from individuals is not only a legal requirement but also an ethical imperative. Consider the analogy of a doctor who collects medical data from patients: while the doctor needs detailed information to diagnose and treat illnesses, there is a strict code of ethics and legal safeguards governing how that data is used, stored, and shared. Similarly, companies implementing Zero Trust should establish clear policies that define what data is collected, how it is used, and under what circumstances it may be shared or retained. These policies should be communicated clearly to all stakeholders and be subject to regular review and updates in response to new legal developments or changes in public sentiment.

International considerations add yet another layer to the legal and regulatory challenges faced by organizations adopting Zero Trust. In a globalized world, companies often operate across multiple jurisdictions, each with its own set of laws and regulations governing data protection and cybersecurity. For instance, while the GDPR imposes strict requirements on data processing and privacy in the European Union, regulations in the United States may be more fragmented, with different states enacting their own rules. An international corporation must therefore design its Zero Trust architecture to be flexible enough to comply with a variety of legal regimes. This could involve implementing localized data storage solutions, varying access controls based on geographic location, or even tailoring monitoring practices to meet different regulatory standards. An analogy for this challenge is like trying to navigate different traffic laws in various countries: while the fundamental goal is the same—safety on the road—the specific rules and regulations can vary widely, and a driver must adapt accordingly.

Organizations must do the same with their security practices, ensuring that their Zero Trust solutions are adaptable and compliant wherever they operate.

The role of ethics in shaping future legal frameworks is also significant. As public awareness of data privacy grows and citizens demand greater control over their personal information, lawmakers are increasingly looking to create legislation that not only punishes breaches but also promotes transparency and accountability. This evolving legal landscape will likely influence how Zero Trust architectures are designed and implemented. In the coming years, we may see new regulations that specifically address the balance between continuous monitoring and individual privacy, or that mandate the use of explainable AI in risk assessment. Organizations that proactively integrate ethical considerations into their Zero Trust frameworks will be better positioned to comply with these future regulations and to build trust with their customers and employees. In many ways, ethics serve as the compass that guides the evolution of legal standards, ensuring that technological progress does not come at the expense of fundamental rights and freedoms.

To further illustrate these points, consider the case of a multinational healthcare provider that implemented a Zero Trust framework across its network of hospitals and clinics. Recognizing that patient data is among the most sensitive information a company can handle, the organization established strict data protection policies that went beyond the minimum legal requirements. Every access attempt to electronic health records was logged, and sophisticated anonymization techniques were employed to ensure that even if logs were accessed, individual patient identities could not be discerned. The organization also implemented strict vendor management policies, requiring all third-party partners to adhere to its high standards for data security and privacy. In parallel, the healthcare provider engaged with regulators and patient advocacy groups to ensure that its practices were transparent and ethically sound. This multi-pronged approach not only reduced the risk of data breaches but also bolstered the organization's reputation as a leader in patient privacy and data protection—a critical asset in an industry where trust is paramount.

Another illustrative example comes from the financial services sector, where a prominent bank was compelled to overhaul its security practices after several high-profile breaches. The bank's existing security measures, which relied heavily on static controls and periodic audits, were found to be inadequate in the face of sophisticated cyberattacks. In response, the bank adopted a Zero Trust model that required continuous authentication and real-time risk assessment for every transaction. Recognizing the legal implications of collecting vast amounts of personal data for security purposes, the bank implemented strict data minimization policies and robust encryption techniques to protect sensitive information. The bank also established an internal ethics board to review its monitoring practices and ensure they did not infringe on customer privacy. Through this approach, the bank not only enhanced its security posture but also built a framework that balanced the need for rigorous security with the legal and ethical imperative to protect personal data.

The discussion of legal, regulatory, and ethical considerations in Zero Trust also extends to the accountability mechanisms that must be in place. In an ideal Zero Trust environment, every access request and security decision is logged, creating an auditable trail that can be used in legal proceedings or regulatory audits. This level of accountability is analogous to maintaining detailed financial records in a business; just as accurate bookkeeping is essential for tax compliance and financial transparency, comprehensive security logs are essential for demonstrating compliance with data protection regulations. However, this accountability comes with its own challenges. The sheer volume of data generated by continuous monitoring can be overwhelming, and organizations must ensure that these logs are managed in a secure and compliant manner. Advanced analytics and automated retention policies can help manage this data, but they must be designed in accordance with legal requirements for data storage and deletion. For example, certain regulations may mandate that logs be retained for a specific period, while others may require that data be purged after a defined time to protect individual privacy. Balancing these requirements is a complex task that requires close collaboration between legal, IT, and compliance teams.

The ethical dimension of accountability also involves ensuring that security practices are fair and do not lead to unintended consequences. One ethical concern is the potential for over-surveillance, where continuous monitoring becomes so intrusive that it erodes trust and creates a culture of fear. An analogy can be drawn to a society where every citizen is under constant surveillance by the government—while such measures might deter criminal activity, they also risk stifling freedom of expression and innovation. In the corporate world, employees who feel excessively monitored may become disengaged or even attempt to bypass security measures, inadvertently increasing the risk of breaches. Therefore, organizations must strike a balance between ensuring accountability and preserving a culture of trust and autonomy. This might involve limiting the granularity of monitoring in certain contexts, providing clear communication about what data is collected and why, and implementing robust safeguards to prevent misuse of monitoring data.

As the legal and regulatory landscape evolves, organizations must also prepare for the possibility of new standards that specifically address the challenges posed by Zero Trust. Emerging areas such as data ethics, algorithmic transparency, and digital identity management are likely to become the focus of future legislation. Companies that invest in ethical design and transparent practices today will be better positioned to adapt to these changes. For example, developing an explainable AI system for risk assessment within a Zero Trust framework not only improves trust among users but also anticipates future regulatory requirements that may mandate transparency in automated decision-making. By proactively aligning their practices with emerging legal and ethical standards, organizations can mitigate the risk of non-compliance and demonstrate leadership in responsible innovation.

In summary, the integration of legal, regulatory, and ethical considerations into the Zero Trust framework is a multifaceted challenge that requires a comprehensive and nuanced approach. Organizations must navigate a complex regulatory landscape that governs data privacy, security, and accountability while also addressing ethical concerns related to continuous monitoring, bias, and over-surveillance. Real-world examples—from healthcare providers safeguarding patient data to financial institutions overhauling their security practices—demonstrate that it is possible to build robust, compliant, and ethical Zero Trust systems. Analogies, such as comparing a Zero Trust environment to a highly secure bank or a medieval castle with multiple layers of defense, help illustrate the importance of layered security and continuous verification.

Ultimately, the future success of Zero Trust will depend not only on technological innovation but also on the ability of organizations to align their security practices with the evolving legal and ethical norms of society. By fostering transparency, engaging with stakeholders, and continuously refining policies in response to new challenges, companies can create Zero Trust environments that are not only secure and resilient but also fair, accountable, and respectful of individual rights. As digital ecosystems become increasingly complex and globalized, this balanced approach will be essential for sustaining trust in the digital age.

CHAPTER 12: INCIDENT RESPONSE AND RECOVERY IN A ZERO TRUST ENVIRONMENT

In a world where cyber threats are evolving at breakneck speed and the digital landscape is constantly in flux, no security strategy can be considered complete without a robust plan for incident response and recovery. Zero Trust is built on the idea that no user, device, or system should be trusted by default, which means that even the most secure environments must be prepared for the inevitability of a breach. In this chapter, we explore how organizations can build an incident response and recovery framework within a Zero Trust environment. We delve into the planning, execution, and iterative improvement processes that underpin a rapid, effective response to cyberattacks, and we illustrate these concepts with real-world examples and relatable analogies.

Imagine a high-tech, modern fortress that is continuously monitored and fortified at every level. No matter how strong the outer walls, history has taught us that determined adversaries can sometimes breach the defenses. In this analogy, the fortress represents an organization's digital environment built on Zero Trust principles, and the adversaries are the cybercriminals. Incident response and recovery, then, are like the internal emergency systems of that fortress—fire alarms, sprinklers, and rapid-response teams that quickly isolate, contain, and neutralize any threat that manages to get inside. This is the mindset required when designing incident response strategies for a Zero Trust environment.

The first step in developing a successful incident response strategy is meticulous planning. Organizations must assume that, despite every precaution, a breach is not a matter of if, but when. This mindset compels them to build a comprehensive response plan that encompasses every stage of the incident lifecycle—from detection and analysis to containment, eradication, and recovery. A key element of this planning is a detailed understanding of the organization's digital assets. Much like an emergency evacuation plan for a large building requires a map of all exits and corridors, an incident response plan must begin with an exhaustive inventory of hardware, software, user accounts, data flows, and access points. In a Zero Trust environment, where every interaction is continually verified, this inventory forms the backbone of the response plan, enabling security teams to quickly identify which systems have been compromised and how the breach might propagate through micro-segments.

For instance, consider a medium-sized financial institution that adopted Zero Trust to secure its sensitive customer data. Prior to implementation, the bank performed a detailed asset mapping exercise. Every server, workstation, mobile device, and even IoT device such as ATMs and digital kiosks were cataloged, and their interconnections were documented. When an anomaly was later detected in the network—an unusual pattern of access to customer data from one branch office—the bank's incident response team was able to quickly trace the access path through its segmented network. Because of the granular visibility provided by the Zero Trust framework, they identified that a single compromised workstation had served as a pivot point. This allowed them to isolate the segment, contain the breach, and prevent lateral movement to other critical systems. Such preparedness not only limited potential damages but also provided clear evidence to regulators, thereby reducing legal and financial liabilities.

Once a breach is detected, the next critical phase is containment. In a Zero Trust environment, containment strategies are both more granular and more dynamic than in traditional security models. The principle of "never trust, always verify" ensures that every interaction is evaluated continuously. When a threat is detected, the system can automatically enforce segmentation policies to isolate affected devices or network zones. This is similar to a ship's watertight compartments that prevent a single breach from sinking the entire vessel. In our financial institution example, once the compromised workstation was identified, automated security policies kicked in to lock down the affected segment. This rapid containment prevented the attacker from moving laterally within the network and gaining access to additional sensitive data. Containment also involves communication protocols that quickly alert key stakeholders, such as the IT security team, senior management, and, where appropriate, external partners like law enforcement or regulatory bodies.

In many cases, containment is achieved through automation. Modern Zero Trust architectures integrate advanced endpoint detection and response (EDR) systems that work in real time. These systems monitor behavioral patterns and system integrity, flagging any deviation from the norm. When an incident occurs, the orchestration of automated responses —such as revoking access credentials, isolating a network segment, or even shutting down compromised endpoints— ensures that the spread of a breach is halted swiftly. Imagine a factory floor where a single machine malfunctions and triggers an automated shutdown of a production line, preventing defective products from moving further down the line. This is the type of precision containment that automated security tools can deliver in a Zero Trust environment.

Following containment, the next phase in the incident response lifecycle is eradication and recovery. Eradication involves the removal of the threat from the environment, which may include cleaning malware, patching vulnerabilities, or removing unauthorized access points. Recovery then focuses on restoring normal operations and ensuring that all systems are back to their secure baseline state. In a Zero Trust model, recovery is not simply a matter of "fixing" the compromised systems; it is an opportunity to reapply the core principles of Zero Trust and learn from the incident. For example, after the financial institution isolated and eradicated the compromised workstation, its IT team conducted a thorough post-incident review. They analyzed logs, correlated data from various security sensors, and identified gaps in their existing policies. As a result, they refined their authentication protocols, tightened segmentation rules, and updated their incident response playbooks. Recovery in this sense is an iterative process—each incident provides valuable feedback that strengthens the overall security posture.

A practical analogy for recovery is the process of rehabilitating a patient after surgery. Just as doctors monitor vital signs, adjust medications, and provide rehabilitative care to ensure the patient returns to full health, security teams must monitor their systems post-incident, apply patches and updates, and sometimes even reconfigure network settings to ensure that vulnerabilities are not left behind. The success of recovery is measured not only by how quickly operations are restored but also by the lessons learned and the improvements made to prevent similar incidents in the future.

Incident response in a Zero Trust environment also relies heavily on the integration of continuous monitoring and real-time analytics. With traditional security models, incident response often relied on periodic reviews of logs and manual investigations—a process that could take hours or even days. In contrast, Zero Trust architectures are designed to provide a constant stream of data that can be analyzed in real time. Advanced machine learning algorithms sift through vast amounts of telemetry data from endpoints, network traffic, and application logs to identify even the most subtle anomalies. For instance, a retail company with an integrated Zero Trust system might detect a slight deviation in the behavior of an employee's login pattern—perhaps a slight change in typing speed or unusual navigation between sensitive internal systems. This seemingly minor anomaly could be an early warning sign of an insider threat or compromised credentials. Real-time analytics would flag this behavior immediately, prompting a deeper investigation and, if necessary, triggering automated containment measures. By catching incidents early in their development, organizations can prevent small issues from evolving into full-blown breaches.

Real-world examples provide further clarity on the value of a well-integrated incident response strategy within a Zero Trust framework. Consider a large government agency that faced a sophisticated cyberattack aimed at its classified data repositories. Despite having state-of-the-art defenses, the attackers managed to breach one segment of the network through a phishing campaign that compromised an employee's credentials. However, because the agency had implemented Zero Trust principles, the attacker's movement was immediately restricted to a single, isolated zone. The continuous monitoring systems detected irregular access patterns, and within minutes, automated containment protocols were activated. The agency's incident response team, armed with comprehensive logs and real-time data, was able to trace the origin of the breach, patch the vulnerability, and restore normal operations. The entire episode was documented meticulously, and the lessons learned led to an overhaul of the agency's security policies—ensuring that future incidents would be even less likely to succeed. This case exemplifies how a Zero Trust approach transforms a potential disaster into a manageable incident, limiting damage and accelerating recovery.

Another illustrative example comes from the world of e-commerce. A rapidly growing online retailer, which had embraced Zero Trust to secure its customer data and payment systems, encountered an attack that exploited a previously unknown vulnerability in one of its web applications. The attack was detected by the retailer's continuous monitoring system, which immediately alerted the security operations center. Automated scripts were deployed to isolate the affected micro-segment, effectively quarantining the compromised application from the rest of the network. Meanwhile, the incident response team launched a full-scale investigation, analyzing logs and cross-referencing user activity to pinpoint the origin of the breach. Within a few hours, the vulnerability was identified, patched, and the affected systems were reintegrated into the network. The entire incident, while initially alarming, ended up being a valuable learning experience. The retailer updated its development protocols to include additional security testing, and its Zero Trust framework was refined to further reduce the risk of similar attacks. This example shows how even in the high-stakes world of online retail, where customer trust is paramount, a Zero Trust incident response strategy can quickly neutralize threats and bolster long-term security.

An important analogy for understanding the dynamics of incident response in a Zero Trust environment is that of a well-coordinated emergency response system in a major city. When a fire breaks out, it is not enough to simply have a robust fire department; the city must have a comprehensive emergency plan that includes early detection systems, clearly defined communication channels, rapid containment strategies, and well-practiced recovery procedures. Every second counts, and the response must be both immediate and well-coordinated to prevent the fire from spreading. In a Zero Trust environment, the "fire" is a cyberattack, and the "fire department" consists of automated security systems, real-time analytics, and a dedicated incident response team. Just as a city's emergency response plan is constantly updated based on lessons learned from previous incidents, the incident response protocols in a Zero Trust framework are continuously refined to address new threats. This analogy underscores that effective incident response is not a static plan but a dynamic, evolving process that requires ongoing attention and adaptation.

Developing an incident response plan in a Zero Trust environment also means establishing clear roles and responsibilities. Every member of the organization—from front-line IT staff to senior management—must know what to do when an incident occurs. This clarity is achieved through detailed playbooks, regular training exercises, and simulated cyberattacks designed to test the response plan under realistic conditions. For example, a mid-sized manufacturing firm might conduct biannual "cyber fire drills" in which simulated breaches are introduced into the system. These exercises not only test the technical response capabilities but also the communication protocols among different departments. By identifying bottlenecks and areas of confusion during these drills, the organization can refine its procedures and ensure that everyone knows their role when a real incident occurs. In this way, the process of training and simulation builds organizational resilience—much like how regular fire drills in a school prepare students and staff to respond effectively in an emergency.

Recovery is perhaps the most critical phase of the incident response lifecycle. Once the threat is contained and eradicated, the focus shifts to restoring normal operations and learning from the incident. Recovery in a Zero Trust environment involves not only technical remediation—such as patching vulnerabilities and restoring data from backups—but also a comprehensive post-incident analysis. This analysis should document what happened, how the breach was detected, how effectively the containment measures worked, and what improvements can be made to prevent future incidents. A useful analogy here is that of a sports team reviewing game footage after a loss. Coaches and players examine every play to understand what went wrong, adjust strategies, and improve performance for the next game. Similarly, organizations must conduct thorough "post-mortems" after each incident, using the insights gained to refine their Zero Trust policies, update their security controls, and bolster their incident response plans.

In one notable case, a global technology firm experienced a significant breach that exploited a misconfigured cloud storage bucket. Although the breach was contained quickly by the firm's Zero Trust systems—preventing unauthorized access to critical systems—the recovery phase was intensive. The incident response team worked around the clock to analyze the breach, determine its impact, and restore data from secure backups. They also conducted an extensive review of their cloud configurations and discovered that similar misconfigurations existed in other parts of the network. As a result, the firm not only corrected the immediate issue but also implemented a comprehensive audit process for all cloud resources. This proactive approach to recovery ensured that the same vulnerability could not be exploited again, and it served as a catalyst for broader improvements in the firm's overall security posture.

It is also essential for organizations to consider the human element in incident response and recovery. Cybersecurity is not just about technology—it is about people, processes, and communication. A breach can create significant stress and uncertainty among employees, potentially undermining confidence and morale. Transparent communication during and after an incident is critical for maintaining trust within the organization. For example, after a data breach at a regional healthcare provider, management held a series of town hall meetings to explain what had happened, what steps were being taken to address the issue, and what measures would be implemented to prevent future incidents. This openness not only helped to alleviate employee concerns but also reinforced a culture of collective responsibility for security. In a Zero Trust environment, where continuous monitoring and verification are the norm, maintaining human trust is as important as technological resilience.

The financial and reputational costs of a cyber incident can be enormous, particularly for organizations that fail to recover quickly. By investing in robust incident response and recovery mechanisms as part of their Zero Trust strategy, organizations can minimize downtime, reduce legal and regulatory penalties, and protect their brand reputation. An analogy for this investment is like having comprehensive insurance for a valuable asset. While no one wants to experience a loss, knowing that there is a plan in place to quickly restore operations can make the difference between a minor setback and a catastrophic failure. For SMEs and large enterprises alike, the costs associated with proactive incident response are far outweighed by the potential losses from an uncontained breach.

Looking ahead, the future of incident response in a Zero Trust environment will be shaped by ongoing technological advances. As artificial intelligence, machine learning, and automation continue to mature, we can expect incident response systems to become even more predictive and preemptive. Rather than reacting to breaches after they occur, future systems may be able to anticipate potential threats and take preemptive measures. Imagine a scenario where a system detects subtle shifts in user behavior that historically have preceded a breach; it could automatically adjust access privileges or trigger targeted security checks before an actual incident occurs. This level of proactive defense would further minimize risk and enhance the overall resilience of the organization.

Furthermore, the integration of emerging technologies such as blockchain could revolutionize how incident response and recovery data is stored and shared. Blockchain's immutable ledger capabilities could provide a tamper-proof record of every access attempt, every security alert, and every remediation step taken during an incident. This would not only aid in forensic investigations but also build a transparent history that can be audited by regulators and trusted by stakeholders. In a future where data breaches are a constant risk, having a reliable, decentralized record of security events could become an invaluable asset, reinforcing the integrity of the Zero Trust model.

Collaboration will remain a cornerstone of successful incident response strategies. No organization can tackle cyber threats in isolation. As cyberattacks become more sophisticated and cross-border in nature, sharing threat intelligence and best practices will be essential. Many industries have already established information-sharing and analysis centers (ISACs) where members collaborate to identify emerging threats and develop coordinated responses. In a Zero Trust context, such collaboration is even more critical, as real-time data on breaches and attack vectors can help organizations adjust their defenses on the fly. For example, if several organizations in the same sector report similar anomalous behavior on their networks, this information can be shared through an ISAC, prompting all members to review their incident response protocols and apply necessary patches. This collective vigilance creates a community defense, where the lessons learned from one incident contribute to the overall security of the industry.

In conclusion, incident response and recovery in a Zero Trust environment is an ongoing, dynamic process that demands meticulous planning, rapid execution, and continuous improvement. The principles of Zero Trust—continuous verification, granular access controls, and dynamic risk assessment—extend beyond the prevention of breaches; they form the foundation for a resilient, adaptive response when breaches do occur. Through detailed asset mapping, automated containment strategies, rigorous post-incident analyses, and a culture of transparency and collaboration, organizations can not only limit the damage of cyberattacks but also emerge stronger and more secure.

The journey from detection to recovery is akin to the operations of a high-functioning emergency response team: every moment is critical, every decision must be informed by real-time data, and every lesson learned becomes a building block for future resilience. Just as a city's emergency services are continually trained, upgraded, and refined to meet new challenges, so too must an organization's incident response and recovery processes evolve. With the proper blend of technology, human expertise, and procedural rigor, the Zero Trust model transforms potential disasters into manageable incidents—and each incident, no matter how severe, becomes an opportunity for improvement.

Ultimately, the goal of incident response in a Zero Trust environment is not merely to restore normal operations after an attack but to build an organizational culture where continuous vigilance, learning, and adaptation are the norm. By embracing the inevitability of breaches, planning for rapid containment, and investing in effective recovery processes, organizations can ensure that every digital breach is met with a measured, strategic, and ultimately successful response. This holistic approach—where technology, processes, and people work together seamlessly—represents the future of cybersecurity in an increasingly complex digital landscape.

In a world where threats are ever-present and the only constant is change, organizations that invest in robust incident response and recovery strategies will not only safeguard their assets but also reinforce the trust of their stakeholders. Zero Trust, with its relentless commitment to "never trust, always verify," offers the ideal framework for this continuous battle against cyber adversaries. Like a well-drilled fire brigade that responds to every spark with precision and coordination, a well-implemented Zero Trust incident response system stands ready to protect, contain, and recover from even the most sophisticated cyberattacks.

As we look to the future, the evolution of incident response in a Zero Trust environment promises to be as transformative as the paradigm itself. With advances in automation, artificial intelligence, blockchain, and collaborative intelligence, the processes of detection, containment, and recovery will become faster, more precise, and even more integrated into the day-to-day operations of organizations. This evolution will ensure that when breaches do occur, they are not catastrophic events but rather isolated incidents that are swiftly and effectively managed—turning every challenge into an opportunity to enhance resilience and build a more secure digital future.

In summary, a robust incident response and recovery strategy within a Zero Trust framework is essential for any organization operating in today's high-risk digital environment. It requires a comprehensive, well-documented plan; advanced technologies for continuous monitoring and automated response; a culture of proactive training and transparency; and, above all, the willingness to learn from each incident to build a stronger defense. With these elements in place, organizations can ensure that even when cyber threats slip past their front-line defenses, they are prepared to contain the damage, restore operations, and emerge even more secure than before.

CHAPTER 13: BUILDING A ZERO TRUST SECURITY CULTURE

In the rapidly evolving world of cybersecurity, technology alone cannot ensure protection against sophisticated cyber threats. The true strength of a Zero Trust framework lies not only in firewalls, multi-factor authentication, or continuous monitoring, but in cultivating a culture in which every individual within the organization is an active participant in security. Building a Zero Trust security culture means transforming the mindset of employees and leadership alike, embedding security as a core value in every process and decision, and ensuring that every user—from the CEO to a new intern—understands that trust must be continuously earned. In this chapter, we explore how organizations can build such a culture by discussing the challenges of cultural change, examining effective training programs and communication strategies, and offering real-world examples and analogies that illustrate the journey from traditional practices to a resilient Zero Trust culture.

At its heart, a Zero Trust security culture is about shifting from a mindset of "if you're inside, you're safe" to one where every access, action, and communication is treated as potentially untrustworthy until verified. This transformation requires a fundamental change in how people think about security. In many organizations, security has historically been seen as the sole responsibility of the IT department—a necessary but distant function that doesn't affect daily work. However, in a Zero Trust environment, security is everyone's business. Every employee must assume a role akin to that of a vigilant guard at every door and window of a fortress, ensuring that no one is allowed in without the proper credentials and continuous re-verification.

Consider an analogy: imagine a medieval castle. In traditional times, the castle's defenses were built around a massive, thick wall that was meant to keep invaders out. Once inside the walls, however, trust was assumed—knights, servants, and residents moved freely without additional checks. In a modern Zero Trust environment, the castle has been completely reimagined. Now, every door, gate, and passageway is locked and requires a passcode or biometric scan for entry, no matter who you are or where you're coming from. Even if someone gains entry to one room, they are not automatically granted access to the entire castle. This analogy illustrates how a Zero Trust culture does not rely on a single, impenetrable barrier but on a network of continuous, dynamic checks. Each employee, much like each door in the castle, becomes a checkpoint for security.

The first step in building a Zero Trust culture is leadership commitment. Transformation begins at the top. Leaders must recognize that cybersecurity is not just a technical challenge but a strategic imperative that impacts every aspect of the business. When executives visibly champion security initiatives and integrate them into the organization's mission and values, employees are more likely to adopt and internalize these practices. For instance, if a CEO holds regular town hall meetings focused on security updates and explains how every team member contributes to protecting the organization, the message resonates throughout the company. Leadership should set clear expectations, allocate resources for training and technology, and ensure that policies are aligned with the Zero Trust model. Just as a captain's calm and determined demeanor can inspire confidence in a ship's crew during a storm, leadership that demonstrates a genuine commitment to security will foster a culture where every employee is alert and accountable.

Organizational change management is a critical component of this cultural transformation. Many employees are naturally resistant to change, especially when new practices seem to add complexity to their daily routines. Changing long-established habits is challenging. One effective strategy is to implement change gradually. Rather than imposing a radical, all-at-once shift, organizations can start with pilot programs or small-scale initiatives that illustrate the benefits of Zero Trust practices. For example, an IT department might begin by applying continuous verification to a single critical application or segment of the network. As employees observe that these changes lead to fewer security incidents and improved system performance, they become more open to broader implementation. This incremental approach is similar to the way a chef might perfect one dish before expanding the menu; small, successful experiments build confidence and pave the way for larger-scale adoption.

Training and awareness programs are fundamental to building a Zero Trust culture. Employees must be educated not only on the technical aspects of new security tools but also on the underlying philosophy of continuous verification. Comprehensive training programs should cover topics such as recognizing phishing attempts, the importance of strong, unique passwords, and the reasons behind multi-factor authentication. Real-world examples are particularly effective. For instance, a case study involving a mid-sized law firm might illustrate how a single phishing email led to a data breach because an employee inadvertently provided access credentials. By contrasting that incident with another scenario where proper training and adherence to Zero Trust protocols prevented a breach, employees can see the direct benefits of following the new rules. Workshops, interactive sessions, and even simulated cyberattacks can create a dynamic learning environment where employees gain practical experience and understand the importance of each security measure.

Analogies are useful tools in training as well. Think of cybersecurity as a personal fitness regimen. Just as a healthy lifestyle requires regular exercise, balanced nutrition, and consistent sleep, a strong security posture requires continuous effort—regular password updates, routine device checks, and constant vigilance against suspicious activities. Employees who understand that security is like physical fitness are more likely to integrate those practices into their daily lives. Over time, just as regular exercise leads to improved health and resilience, continuous adherence to security protocols leads to a more robust defense against cyber threats.

Communication plays a vital role in maintaining a Zero Trust culture. It is essential that the objectives and benefits of Zero Trust are communicated clearly across the organization. Regular updates about security measures, incidents, and improvements help keep everyone informed and engaged. For example, an organization might publish monthly security newsletters that highlight recent trends, share success stories from the incident response team, and provide tips for everyday vigilance. Visual dashboards and infographics can make data more accessible, turning abstract security metrics into concrete information that employees can relate to. In one case, a manufacturing company used a live security dashboard displayed in the common area of its main office. This dashboard showed real-time statistics on attempted intrusions, successful verifications, and the overall health of the network. Employees began to see security not as a distant IT issue but as a tangible, integral part of the company's operations. By demystifying security data and involving everyone in the conversation, organizations can foster a sense of shared responsibility and empowerment.

A key challenge in building a Zero Trust culture is overcoming the "us versus them" mentality that can develop between IT/security teams and other departments. In some organizations, there is a perception that security measures are imposed from above without regard for operational realities, leading to friction and even resentment. To address this, it is important to involve representatives from all areas of the organization in the planning and implementation of security policies. Cross-functional teams can collaborate to develop protocols that are both secure and practical. For instance, a retail chain might form a committee that includes members from IT, operations, sales, and customer service to review and refine access controls and security policies. This collaborative approach ensures that security measures are tailored to the specific needs of each department while reinforcing the idea that security is a collective responsibility. When employees see that their voices are heard and that security measures are designed with their input, they are more likely to embrace the changes rather than view them as burdensome impositions.

Incentivizing security-conscious behavior is another strategy for cultivating a Zero Trust culture. Organizations can develop recognition programs, bonuses, or other rewards for employees who demonstrate exemplary adherence to security protocols. For example, an insurance company might launch a "Security Star" program where employees who report phishing attempts or suggest effective security improvements are publicly recognized and rewarded. Such initiatives not only motivate individuals to follow best practices but also create positive peer pressure, encouraging others to adopt the same mindset. An analogy can be drawn to a sports team, where each player's performance contributes to the overall success of the team. Just as coaches reward players for outstanding teamwork and adherence to the game plan, organizations can reward employees who contribute to the security of the company, reinforcing that every role is vital in maintaining a robust defense.

Measurement and feedback are essential components of building a Zero Trust security culture. Without metrics, it is difficult to know whether the cultural shift is taking root or if additional interventions are needed. Organizations can use surveys, incident reports, and security audits to gauge employee awareness, engagement, and compliance. For example, after launching a new training program, a company might conduct anonymous surveys to assess whether employees understand the Zero Trust model and how it applies to their daily tasks. Over time, a decrease in security incidents, along with improved survey scores, can indicate that the culture is shifting in the desired direction. Regular feedback loops allow organizations to adjust their training and communication strategies, ensuring that the culture continues to evolve and improve.

Technology itself can be a facilitator of cultural change. For instance, gamification of security training has proven effective in engaging employees. A technology firm might create an online game or simulation where employees must complete challenges related to identifying phishing emails, securing endpoints, or responding to simulated breaches. By turning learning into an interactive and competitive experience, the organization not only makes security training more enjoyable but also reinforces the importance of vigilance in a memorable way. Employees who might otherwise be indifferent to mandatory training sessions become active participants, and the lessons learned in the game can translate into real-world behavior. Such innovative approaches are especially valuable in industries where traditional training methods may fail to capture the interest of a diverse workforce.

Real-world examples provide valuable insights into how a Zero Trust culture can be successfully established. One notable case involved a multinational technology company that was facing increasing threats from both external hackers and insider threats. Recognizing that technology alone would not suffice, the company launched a comprehensive cultural transformation initiative centered on Zero Trust principles. Leadership took the initiative by hosting town hall meetings, where the CEO and other executives explained the importance of continuous verification and the shared responsibility for security. They also invested in extensive training programs that used real-life scenarios to illustrate the impact of security breaches and the value of proactive defense. Over time, the company saw not only a reduction in security incidents but also an improvement in overall employee engagement and a sense of collective ownership over the company's digital safety. Employees began to refer to their computers as "their little fortresses," each one requiring a passcode, multi-factor authentication, and regular security updates—much like a medieval knight who must secure every door before entering a castle. This transformation was so successful that the company's approach was later adopted as a model for industry best practices, demonstrating the far-reaching impact of building a robust Zero Trust security culture.

An analogy that resonates well with building a Zero Trust culture is the concept of community policing. In traditional policing, officers are often seen as external enforcers, stepping in only when crimes occur. However, community policing involves every citizen in maintaining public safety—neighbors watch out for one another, share information, and collectively work to prevent crime. In a Zero Trust culture, every employee is like a community member who is vigilant and engaged. They understand that their actions matter, that they have the power to notice and report anomalies, and that together, they create an environment where trust is earned through constant, collective effort. This analogy highlights that a successful Zero Trust culture is not built solely on technology but on the active participation and collaboration of everyone in the organization.

Another important aspect is the integration of security into everyday business processes. Often, security is viewed as an extra layer that slows down operations. However, when integrated seamlessly into daily routines, it becomes a natural part of the workflow. For example, a mid-sized logistics company revamped its shipment tracking system to incorporate continuous authentication and access controls. Instead of treating security as a separate, cumbersome process, the system required employees to authenticate using a mobile app that verified their identity and device status before accessing sensitive data. Over time, the employees became accustomed to the process, and it even improved efficiency by reducing unauthorized access and streamlining incident response. This integration demonstrates that security can, and should, be an enabler rather than an obstacle—much like seat belts in a car, which initially may seem inconvenient but ultimately save lives and enhance safety without compromising comfort.

Challenges are inevitable when attempting to shift an organizational culture. Resistance to change is one of the most common hurdles. Employees accustomed to traditional practices may perceive new security protocols as intrusive or burdensome. Overcoming this resistance requires transparent communication, empathy, and, in many cases, incentives that make the transition smoother. Change management specialists recommend involving employees early in the process, soliciting feedback, and iteratively refining procedures based on real-world experience. Just as a sports team may adjust its strategy based on the strengths and weaknesses of its players, organizations must tailor their security culture initiatives to suit the unique dynamics of their workforce.

Measurement of cultural change is critical. It is important to establish clear metrics and regularly assess progress. These metrics might include the frequency of security incidents, employee participation in training programs, survey results regarding security awareness, and even qualitative feedback from focus groups. A financial services firm, for example, might track the number of phishing attempts reported by employees or measure the reduction in unauthorized access events over time. These data points serve as both benchmarks for success and tools for continuous improvement. When employees see that their efforts lead to measurable improvements in security, they are more likely to remain engaged and proactive.

A further analogy can be drawn from the world of gardening.

Cultivating a Zero Trust culture is similar to tending a garden. It requires regular care, attention, and adaptation to changing conditions. Just as a gardener must prepare the soil, plant seeds, water regularly, and remove weeds, organizational leaders must prepare the groundwork through education and training, nurture security awareness, continuously monitor the environment, and prune practices that no longer serve the collective good. Over time, this nurturing results in a thriving, resilient garden—a workplace where security is deeply ingrained in the fabric of everyday activities. Just as a garden that is well-tended bears fruit, an organization with a strong security culture reaps benefits in the form of reduced incidents, higher employee morale, and improved overall resilience.

Technological tools can further support this cultural shift by making security practices more accessible and engaging. For example, gamified security training modules, interactive dashboards, and mobile apps for reporting suspicious activity transform abstract security policies into tangible, everyday actions. Employees who might otherwise view security measures as an inconvenience come to see them as tools that empower them to protect not just corporate assets but also their personal digital lives. In one case study, a small marketing agency introduced a points-based system for employees who completed security training modules and reported potential threats. Over time, the initiative led to a measurable improvement in security posture and even sparked friendly competition among teams, reinforcing the idea that everyone's contribution is vital to maintaining a secure environment.

Another element crucial to building a Zero Trust security culture is aligning performance metrics and incentives with security goals. In many organizations, success is measured solely by operational metrics such as sales numbers or production output, with little regard for security performance. By incorporating security into performance evaluations and providing tangible rewards for adherence to security protocols, organizations signal that security is not an optional add-on but a core component of success. For example, a regional hospital might include cybersecurity awareness and adherence to security policies as part of its annual performance reviews. Employees who consistently follow best practices, report potential vulnerabilities, or contribute to the improvement of security procedures are recognized and rewarded. This alignment of incentives ensures that security becomes a shared priority across the organization.

Finally, building a Zero Trust security culture is an ongoing journey rather than a one-time project. As technology, threats, and organizational structures evolve, so too must the security culture. Continuous improvement processes, regular training updates, and adaptive policies are essential to maintain momentum. Organizations should view every security incident as an opportunity to learn and grow. Post-incident reviews, for instance, are not merely about assigning blame but about understanding the root causes and reinforcing the culture of continuous verification. This iterative process is akin to how athletes review game footage to improve their performance; by analyzing what went wrong and what could be done better, the organization strengthens its defenses for the future.

In conclusion, building a Zero Trust security culture is a multifaceted endeavor that integrates leadership commitment, effective communication, comprehensive training, and the continuous measurement of progress. It is a cultural transformation that requires every individual in the organization to understand that security is a shared responsibility. Through real-world examples, practical analogies, and a commitment to continuous improvement, organizations can shift from outdated, perimeter-based models to a dynamic, resilient culture where every interaction is verified, and every individual plays a role in safeguarding the digital ecosystem.

Just as a fortress is only as strong as the vigilance of its guards, a Zero Trust culture is only as robust as the collective commitment of its people. By embracing the principles of continuous verification, transparent communication, and shared responsibility, organizations can create an environment where trust is continuously earned and every action is an opportunity to strengthen security. This cultural foundation not only minimizes risk but also enhances operational efficiency, builds customer confidence, and positions the organization for long-term success in an increasingly complex digital world.

Ultimately, the journey toward a Zero Trust security culture is as much about transforming hearts and minds as it is about deploying technology. It is about creating a workplace where security is woven into the fabric of everyday life—a place where every employee understands that their actions contribute to the safety of the organization and where leadership sets the tone for a proactive, vigilant, and collaborative approach to cybersecurity. In this way, building a Zero Trust culture is not just an IT initiative; it is a strategic imperative that can redefine an organization's resilience and pave the way for a secure, agile, and future-proof digital future.

CHAPTER 14: THE ZERO TRUST VENDOR ECOSYSTEM AND FUTURE TRENDS

The evolution of cybersecurity has been marked by a gradual shift away from static, perimeter-based defenses toward models that assume breaches are inevitable and thus require constant vigilance. Among these modern approaches, Zero Trust has emerged as a compelling framework that insists every access request—regardless of origin—must be verified continuously. As organizations around the world increasingly embrace Zero Trust, a robust vendor ecosystem has developed to support this paradigm. In this chapter, we explore the landscape of vendors offering Zero Trust solutions, how they interconnect to form an ecosystem, and the future trends that are set to shape the next generation of cybersecurity. Throughout, we use real-world examples and analogies to illustrate how this ecosystem operates and how organizations can best leverage it.

Imagine a bustling marketplace where every vendor specializes in a unique ingredient, yet each contributes to creating a complete, gourmet meal. One vendor supplies the freshest vegetables, another provides high-quality spices, while yet another delivers artisanal bread. In the world of Zero Trust, each vendor offers a specialized component—be it identity and access management, network segmentation, endpoint security, continuous monitoring, or threat intelligence. Just as the gourmet meal depends on the harmony of its diverse ingredients, a successful Zero Trust strategy relies on the seamless integration of solutions from a diverse vendor ecosystem.

At the heart of the Zero Trust vendor ecosystem is identity and access management (IAM). IAM vendors provide the foundational building blocks for verifying users and devices continuously. For instance, companies like Okta and Microsoft Azure Active Directory offer robust identity solutions that use multi-factor authentication (MFA), behavioral analytics, and risk-based authentication to ensure that only authorized individuals can access sensitive data. Consider a scenario where a regional bank implements an IAM solution to monitor and verify all access attempts. Every time a banker logs into a critical financial system, the IAM system cross-references their credentials, evaluates behavioral patterns, and even checks the health status of the device being used. If the system detects an anomaly—say, an attempt to log in from an unexpected location—it prompts for additional verification steps. This real-time, dynamic approach ensures that even if credentials are compromised, unauthorized access is thwarted. In many ways, IAM is like the security guard at the entrance of a secure building who not only checks IDs but also observes body language and cross-references known patterns before granting entry.

Equally important in the Zero Trust ecosystem is network segmentation and micro-segmentation. Traditional networks often operated with flat architectures where, once inside, an attacker could move laterally with ease. Modern vendors like Illumio, VMware NSX, and Cisco offer solutions that divide the network into multiple, isolated segments. This segmentation ensures that even if an intruder breaches one part of the network, they are confined to a small area and cannot easily access other critical systems. To draw an analogy, imagine a large castle divided into separate, locked towers. Even if a foe gains entry into one tower, they cannot automatically roam free into the other parts of the castle. In practice, a manufacturing company might implement micro-segmentation across its production network so that even if a single sensor or IoT device is compromised, the breach is contained and the rest of the operation remains secure.

Endpoint security is another critical pillar in the Zero Trust model, and a host of vendors are dedicated to protecting endpoints ranging from laptops and smartphones to IoT devices. Vendors such as CrowdStrike, SentinelOne, and Carbon Black have developed advanced endpoint detection and response (EDR) tools that continuously monitor endpoint behavior, flag anomalies, and isolate compromised devices. For example, a global logistics company might deploy an EDR solution across its fleet of delivery vehicles and mobile devices used by field employees. If an endpoint starts exhibiting behavior that deviates from its baseline—like unexpected file modifications or unauthorized software installations—the system can automatically quarantine the device, preventing the potential spread of malware throughout the network. This process is akin to having a team of rapid-response medics on standby who can quickly isolate and treat any injury before it becomes a widespread issue.

Continuous monitoring and threat intelligence vendors form the eyes and ears of a Zero Trust architecture. Companies like Splunk, Sumo Logic, and IBM QRadar aggregate data from various sources—logs, network traffic, user activities—and analyze it in real time. These platforms often integrate machine learning algorithms that learn the "normal" behavior of systems and can detect anomalies that might indicate a breach. Picture a city-wide surveillance system that not only records every movement but also uses artificial intelligence to predict unusual behavior before it escalates into a full-blown crisis. For example, an e-commerce company might use a continuous monitoring solution to detect unusual login patterns or sudden surges in data transfers. When such anomalies occur, automated responses—such as additional authentication challenges or temporary access restrictions—are triggered immediately, thereby mitigating risks before they escalate. These monitoring systems act like an early warning radar, providing actionable intelligence that enables rapid response and recovery.

A relatively newer but increasingly important component in the

Zero Trust vendor ecosystem is encryption and data protection. As organizations deal with ever-growing amounts of data, both at rest and in transit, protecting this information is paramount. Vendors like Symantec, McAfee, and newer players specializing in cloud encryption, such as CipherCloud, offer solutions that encrypt data using advanced algorithms and ensure that keys are managed securely. In a Zero Trust model, encryption serves as the final layer of defense. Even if an intruder bypasses other security measures, the data remains unreadable without the proper decryption keys. Imagine a treasure chest locked with a combination that changes continuously based on sophisticated algorithms; even if someone manages to break in, they would still be confronted with the nearly insurmountable task of cracking the dynamic code.

As we look to future trends, several emerging technologies are poised to further transform the Zero Trust vendor ecosystem. One of the most significant developments is the advent of quantum computing. While quantum computing promises to revolutionize numerous fields, it also poses a threat to current encryption methods. In response, vendors are already working on quantum-resistant algorithms that will secure data against the immense computational power of quantum machines. This evolution is similar to the historical transition from traditional locks to advanced electronic locks in response to improved lock-picking techniques. Organizations that adopt quantum-resistant encryption solutions will be better positioned to protect their data in the decades to come.

Blockchain technology is another area set to impact the Zero Trust ecosystem. Blockchain's decentralized, immutable ledger provides a new way to establish trust and transparency in digital transactions. Some vendors are exploring blockchain-based identity management systems, where every access request is recorded in a tamper-proof ledger. For example, a consortium of banks might deploy a blockchain-based solution to verify interbank transactions, ensuring that every transfer is logged and cannot be altered. This approach not only bolsters security but also enhances auditability and accountability. An analogy for this might be a public bulletin board where every transaction is recorded, and anyone can verify its authenticity, thereby reducing the likelihood of fraudulent activities.

Cloud-native solutions continue to gain traction as more organizations migrate their infrastructure to the cloud. Vendors offering Zero Trust solutions specifically designed for cloud environments are rapidly evolving. Services such as Google BeyondCorp, Microsoft Azure Sentinel, and AWS Identity and Access Management are tailored to provide continuous verification and access control across distributed cloud resources. For instance, a global media company might rely on cloud-native Zero Trust tools to manage access to its digital content repositories, ensuring that every access request is scrutinized, regardless of the geographic location of the user. This level of control is akin to having a virtual passport system that checks credentials at every border crossing, even if the entire journey occurs online.

Interoperability among vendors is another critical trend shaping the future of Zero Trust. As the vendor ecosystem grows, organizations face the challenge of integrating multiple solutions from different providers into a coherent security strategy. Standardization efforts and open APIs are emerging as solutions to this challenge. Vendors are increasingly designing their products to work seamlessly with others, much like different pieces of a jigsaw puzzle that fit together to reveal a complete picture. For example, a large enterprise might integrate its IAM, EDR, and continuous monitoring tools through a unified dashboard that provides a holistic view of the security posture. This interoperability not only simplifies management but also enhances the effectiveness of the Zero Trust model by ensuring that every layer of defense communicates with the others in real time.

Vendor ecosystems are not static; they are dynamic and

subject to rapid innovation. Market consolidation is one trend on the horizon, as larger vendors acquire smaller, specialized companies to enhance their offerings. This consolidation can have both positive and negative effects. On the one hand, it may lead to more integrated, comprehensive solutions that are easier for organizations to deploy and manage. On the other hand, it may reduce the diversity of solutions available and increase dependency on a few major players. For SMEs and larger enterprises alike, the challenge will be to strike a balance between leveraging established, robust solutions and maintaining the flexibility to integrate niche, cutting-edge technologies. An analogy for this process is the evolution of the smartphone industry, where a handful of dominant operating systems now govern a market that once had a plethora of competing platforms. Organizations must be vigilant in ensuring that their security solutions remain agile and adaptable, even as market forces drive consolidation.

In addition to consolidation, another future trend is the increased adoption of Zero Trust as a service (ZTaaS). Just as cloud computing revolutionized the way organizations access IT resources by shifting from capital expenditures to subscription-based models, Zero Trust services are emerging that allow organizations to leverage advanced security frameworks without significant upfront investments. For example, a midsize retail chain might subscribe to a ZTaaS platform that provides continuous identity verification, threat intelligence, and automated incident response, all hosted in the cloud. This approach lowers the barrier to entry for smaller organizations that may not have the resources to build and maintain a comprehensive Zero Trust infrastructure in-house. It's analogous to leasing a fleet of vehicles rather than purchasing them outright—ensuring access to the latest technology without the burdens of maintenance and upgrade costs.

The global regulatory environment will also continue to influence the vendor ecosystem and future trends in Zero

Trust. As governments around the world enact stricter data protection and cybersecurity regulations, vendors must ensure that their solutions not only provide robust security but also facilitate compliance. This trend is likely to spur further innovation in features such as detailed logging, audit trails, and automated compliance reporting. For instance, vendors may develop specialized modules that help organizations meet the requirements of frameworks like GDPR, HIPAA, or PCI DSS by automatically generating compliance reports and alerting administrators to any deviations from regulatory standards. Such innovations not only reduce the burden of compliance but also build greater trust with customers and regulators alike.

Looking ahead, the future of the Zero Trust vendor ecosystem is intrinsically linked to the broader trends in digital transformation. As technologies like artificial intelligence, machine learning, quantum computing, blockchain, and edge computing mature, vendors will need to continuously update and refine their offerings to address emerging threats and opportunities. Organizations that wish to maintain a competitive edge must stay informed about these developments and be prepared to adapt their security strategies accordingly. An analogy here is that of an evolving sports team that must continually adjust its playbook to counter new strategies from opposing teams. Just as a team that refuses to evolve risks being outplayed, an organization that clings to outdated security measures risks being compromised by emerging threats.

The vendor ecosystem will also become more collaborative and integrated, with partnerships and alliances playing a crucial role in delivering comprehensive Zero Trust solutions. Industry consortia and standardization bodies, such as the Zero Trust eXtended (ZTX) framework, are emerging to foster collaboration among vendors. These initiatives encourage the development of interoperable solutions that can be seamlessly integrated into a unified security architecture. For example, a large enterprise might benefit from a solution that integrates a best-in-class IAM system with cutting-edge network segmentation and continuous monitoring tools, all connected via standardized APIs that ensure smooth communication. This collaborative ecosystem not only enhances security but also drives innovation by allowing vendors to build on each other's strengths.

Another important aspect of the future of Zero Trust is the increasing role of managed security service providers (MSSPs) and zero trust consultants. As organizations strive to implement these complex frameworks, many are turning to external experts who specialize in Zero Trust strategy and implementation. MSSPs offer comprehensive services that range from risk assessments and architecture design to continuous monitoring and incident response. This outsourcing of security expertise can be especially valuable for SMEs and organizations that lack large, in-house IT security teams. By leveraging external expertise, companies can accelerate their adoption of Zero Trust while ensuring that they adhere to industry best practices and regulatory standards. This model is similar to how businesses often hire specialized consultants for tax, legal, or financial planning—drawing on expert knowledge to navigate complex landscapes.

Furthermore, vendor innovation is likely to drive improvements in user experience and automation. One common criticism of Zero Trust is that its stringent access controls and continuous verification processes can sometimes slow down operations or create friction for users. Future solutions will likely focus on reducing this friction through intelligent automation and seamless integration with existing workflows. For example, imagine an AI-powered authentication system that learns an employee's routine over time and can automatically grant access when patterns match, yet instantly trigger additional verification if something deviates from the norm. This level of intelligent automation would be akin to a trusted personal assistant who knows your schedule and preferences so well that they can anticipate your needs and streamline your day, while also alerting you if something appears out of place.

As digital transformation continues to reshape industries, the convergence of Zero Trust with emerging digital technologies will only deepen. Edge computing, which involves processing data closer to the source rather than in centralized data centers, will require new approaches to Zero Trust that can operate in decentralized environments. Vendors will need to develop solutions that provide continuous verification at the edge, ensuring that devices in remote or distributed locations are authenticated and monitored just as rigorously as those in a central office. This challenge is similar to ensuring the security of a distributed network of bank ATMs—each machine must be individually secured, yet they all need to work together as part of a larger, coordinated system.

In addition, the rise of the Internet of Behaviors (IoB)—the analysis of data generated by individuals' interactions with technology—will further influence Zero Trust strategies. IoB can provide insights into user behavior patterns, which can then be used to fine-tune risk assessments and access controls. For instance, if an employee consistently logs in from a secure location at specific times, the system might gradually reduce friction for those actions while maintaining stringent checks for any deviations. This evolution will require vendors to integrate behavioral analytics into their Zero Trust platforms, creating more personalized and adaptive security measures. The analogy here might be that of a trusted friend who learns your habits over time and can alert you to unusual behavior—only in this case, the "friend" is an AI system dedicated to safeguarding your digital interactions.

As organizations and vendors continue to navigate this complex landscape, the importance of transparency and ethical practices cannot be overstated. With increasing regulatory scrutiny and growing public awareness of data privacy issues, vendors must ensure that their solutions not only provide robust security but also respect user privacy and operate transparently. This may involve the integration of privacy-enhancing technologies, such as data anonymization and secure multiparty computation, into Zero Trust solutions. By doing so, vendors can help organizations build trust with their customers and stakeholders, ensuring that security measures are implemented ethically and in compliance with evolving legal standards.

In conclusion, the Zero Trust vendor ecosystem is a dynamic, rapidly evolving marketplace where specialized solutions—from identity management and network segmentation to endpoint security and continuous monitoring—come together to form a comprehensive defense against cyber threats. Much like a gourmet meal prepared from the finest ingredients sourced from expert vendors, a successful Zero Trust implementation depends on the seamless integration of multiple, specialized components. As future trends such as quantum computing, blockchain, AI, edge computing, and the Internet of Behaviors continue to emerge, the vendor ecosystem will be challenged to innovate and adapt. The result will be increasingly sophisticated, automated, and user-friendly Zero Trust solutions that not only protect organizations from cyber threats but also facilitate compliance, improve operational efficiency, and build lasting trust with stakeholders.

Through real-world examples and vivid analogies—from the fortified castle with guarded doors to the bustling marketplace of specialized vendors—the future of Zero Trust is depicted as a continuously evolving journey. Organizations must remain agile, informed, and proactive in leveraging the best available technologies and practices. The interplay between vendors, regulatory pressures, and technological innovation will define the next era of cybersecurity. For those who embrace this dynamic ecosystem, the rewards will be significant: a secure, resilient, and adaptable digital environment that stands ready to meet the challenges of tomorrow.

In this ever-changing digital landscape, the vendor ecosystem and future trends in Zero Trust are not static destinations but ongoing processes of innovation and improvement. Much like a river that constantly flows and adapts its course, the Zero Trust ecosystem will continue to evolve as new threats emerge and new solutions are developed. Organizations that invest in this future—by staying informed, collaborating with innovative vendors, and integrating the latest technologies—will be well-positioned to secure their digital assets and build a foundation of trust that endures in the face of uncertainty.

Ultimately, the future of Zero Trust is defined by its ability to adapt to the shifting currents of technology, threat, and regulation. The vendor ecosystem will play a crucial role in shaping this future, offering specialized, interoperable solutions that together create a robust defense mechanism. As organizations navigate this evolving landscape, they must remain committed to continuous verification, integration, and ethical practice. With the right blend of technology, collaboration, and forward-thinking strategy, Zero Trust will not only protect today's digital environments but will also pave the way for a secure, resilient, and innovative tomorrow.

CHAPTER 15: CONCLUSION – THE PATH FORWARD IN A ZERO TRUST WORLD

The journey through the world of Zero Trust has been one of continuous transformation—a voyage that has redefined how we think about cybersecurity, risk, and the very notion of trust in the digital age. As we arrive at the conclusion of this exploration, it becomes clear that the traditional concept of security, with its reliance on static perimeters and implicit trust for those within, is a relic of the past. Today, the digital landscape is dynamic, interconnected, and perpetually evolving, demanding a paradigm where every access request is treated as a potential risk, every device must earn its trust, and every interaction is verified continuously. This conclusion serves not only as a summary of the principles and practices we have discussed but also as a roadmap for moving forward into a future where Zero Trust is not just a model but a strategic foundation for all aspects of modern cybersecurity.

Imagine a vast, bustling metropolis where every building, street, and public space is equipped with its own advanced security systems. In this city, there is no single wall or gate that can protect its inhabitants from every threat. Instead, security is embedded in every element of the urban infrastructure—from sensors on streetlights that monitor traffic flow and detect unusual activity to biometric scanners at every building entrance that ensure only authorized personnel can enter. This city is not built on the assumption that those inside its limits are inherently safe; rather, it operates on the principle that trust must be continuously earned. This vision is at the heart of Zero Trust—a model that demands perpetual vigilance, adaptive controls, and a willingness to challenge the status quo.

Over the course of this book, we have examined the evolution of cybersecurity from the days when organizations built physical walls around their networks to the modern era where digital perimeters are blurred by cloud computing, mobile devices, and remote work. We have seen how traditional defenses, once effective in an isolated world, have become inadequate in a hyper-connected environment where threats can come from anywhere. The evolution of cyber threats, coupled with rapid technological advancements, has made it abundantly clear that the old adage of "if you're inside, you're safe" no longer holds true. Instead, every interaction must be subject to rigorous verification. Just as a modern airport employs multiple layers of security—from biometric checks to real-time surveillance and behavioral analytics—Zero Trust requires that every digital request be scrutinized as if it were coming from an untrusted source.

One of the key takeaways from our exploration is that Zero Trust is not merely a set of technical controls but a holistic philosophy that touches every aspect of an organization. It challenges us to rethink our long-held assumptions about what it means to be secure and compels us to adopt a proactive, rather than reactive, approach to risk management. Consider the analogy of a modern sports team. In the past, teams might have relied on a single star player to carry them through challenging matches. However, contemporary teams are built on the principle of collective strength, where every player, regardless of position, is trained to perform at a high level, and every member is held accountable. Similarly, in a Zero Trust environment, security is a shared responsibility, and every user, device, and application must contribute to a resilient, adaptive defense.

Throughout this book, we have delved into the technical architectures that underpin Zero Trust, such as continuous verification, micro-segmentation, and dynamic access control. We have examined the tools and technologies—from identity and access management systems to advanced analytics and endpoint detection—that make these principles actionable. We have also explored how organizations can plan and strategize their transition to a Zero Trust model, the importance of a robust vendor ecosystem, and the critical role of a security culture that embraces continuous improvement and shared responsibility. Each chapter has contributed to a broader understanding of Zero Trust, illustrating that while the model may be complex, its ultimate goal is simple: to create a digital environment where trust is earned, verified, and never assumed.

In the realm of continuous verification, we learned that every access request—whether initiated by an employee working in a secure office or a remote worker accessing systems from a coffee shop—must be evaluated against a dynamic set of policies that consider a multitude of contextual factors. This is reminiscent of a well-organized orchestra where every instrument, no matter how subtle its sound, is continuously tuned and adjusted to create a harmonious performance. If one instrument falls out of tune, the conductor immediately signals for a correction, ensuring that the overall symphony remains intact. In the same way, Zero Trust systems continuously monitor user behavior, device health, and network conditions, ensuring that any deviation from the norm is swiftly addressed before it can compromise the entire environment.

The principle of least privilege further reinforces this approach by ensuring that every user and device is granted only the minimum access necessary to perform its function. This is much like a chef who only uses the precise amount of an ingredient needed for a dish—too much or too little could ruin the final product. By meticulously controlling access, organizations minimize the potential impact of a breach. Even if an attacker manages to compromise one account, the damage is contained because that account has only limited access to sensitive systems. This granular control is achieved through advanced role-based access control systems, which dynamically adjust permissions based on real-time risk assessments.

Micro-segmentation, another critical pillar of Zero Trust, divides the network into isolated compartments, much like the watertight compartments in a ship. In a traditional ship, a single breach in one compartment could cause catastrophic flooding, but in a segmented ship, each compartment is designed to contain the damage. Similarly, if an attacker gains access to one segment of a Zero Trust network, the breach is confined to that segment, preventing lateral movement and protecting the broader environment. Real-world examples from industries such as finance, healthcare, and manufacturing have demonstrated how micro-segmentation can effectively isolate threats and reduce the overall risk of widespread breaches.

As we look to the future, the journey toward Zero Trust will be defined by continuous innovation and adaptation. Emerging technologies such as artificial intelligence, machine learning, quantum computing, and blockchain will further refine and enhance the Zero Trust model. Imagine a future where every access attempt is evaluated by an AI system that has learned the subtle nuances of user behavior, capable of predicting potential breaches before they occur. This is not science fiction—it is a natural evolution of the Zero Trust paradigm. Quantum-resistant encryption will safeguard data against the next generation of computational threats, ensuring that even as adversaries become more powerful, the security of our digital assets remains uncompromised. Blockchain technology may revolutionize identity management by providing immutable, decentralized logs of every access request, enhancing both transparency and accountability.

The future of Zero Trust is also inextricably linked to the evolving regulatory landscape. Governments and regulatory bodies around the world are increasingly focused on data protection and privacy, and organizations must ensure that their security measures not only protect against cyber threats but also comply with legal and regulatory requirements. This dual mandate is akin to a well-governed city that not only maintains robust physical security but also enforces laws that protect the rights and privacy of its citizens. Organizations that embrace Zero Trust are better positioned to meet these demands by maintaining detailed audit trails, enforcing strict access controls, and ensuring that every data transaction is transparent and accountable.

Cultural transformation is perhaps the most challenging yet the most rewarding aspect of the Zero Trust journey. Technology and processes are vital, but without a security culture that permeates every level of the organization, even the most advanced defenses can fall short. Building a Zero Trust culture means engaging every employee—from the CEO to the newest intern—in a shared commitment to continuous verification and vigilance. It means transforming security from an abstract IT function into a tangible, everyday practice. Consider a community where every member is responsible for watching out for one another. When one person notices something amiss, they alert the community, and together, they maintain a safe environment. In the same way, a Zero Trust culture is built on collective responsibility. Training programs, interactive simulations, and regular security updates are essential for ensuring that every individual understands their role in maintaining a secure digital ecosystem. Real-world examples have shown that organizations with strong security cultures experience fewer breaches and recover more quickly when incidents do occur. Employees who are engaged and aware become the first line of defense, detecting and reporting anomalies before they escalate into serious threats.

The transformation to a Zero Trust world is a continuous process—a journey with no final destination. Cyber threats are always evolving, and the defenses we build today must be adaptable enough to meet the challenges of tomorrow. This perpetual evolution is best understood through the analogy of a river. A river is never static; it flows, changes course, and adapts to obstacles in its path. Similarly, a Zero Trust security posture is not a fixed state but a dynamic process that requires constant monitoring, regular updates, and an unwavering commitment to improvement. Every breach, every near-miss, and every success provides valuable data that can be used to fine-tune security controls and drive innovation. In this way, the journey to Zero Trust is not about achieving perfection—it is about building resilience and being prepared for the unexpected.

Leadership plays a critical role in guiding organizations along this path. The commitment of executives to cybersecurity sets the tone for the entire organization. When leaders allocate resources for cutting-edge technology, invest in comprehensive training programs, and actively participate in security initiatives, they signal to every employee that cybersecurity is a top priority. This top-down commitment creates a ripple effect, fostering a culture where security is deeply embedded in the organization's DNA. Imagine a well-coordinated sports team where the coach not only devises a winning strategy but also inspires the players to perform at their best. In the world of cybersecurity, leadership is that coach, and a strong Zero Trust culture is the result of teamwork, dedication, and a shared commitment to excellence.

Collaboration between departments is equally essential. In many traditional organizations, silos exist between IT, operations, finance, and other departments, often leading to fragmented security practices and gaps in defense. Zero Trust demands an integrated approach where cross-functional teams work together to develop and implement security strategies. This collaboration is akin to an orchestra, where each musician must play in harmony with the others to create a symphony. When IT professionals, security experts, and business leaders share information, coordinate their efforts, and support one another, the result is a cohesive, robust security posture that is greater than the sum of its parts.

Looking to the horizon, the future of Zero Trust promises even greater advancements as new technologies, regulatory shifts, and cultural changes converge. Artificial intelligence and machine learning will become more integral to continuous verification, enabling systems to predict and counter threats before they materialize. Quantum computing will necessitate new encryption techniques, ensuring that our data remains secure even as computational power grows exponentially. Blockchain technology may offer novel ways to create tamper-proof records of every access and transaction, further enhancing transparency and accountability. These advancements will not only strengthen our defenses but also create new opportunities for innovation and growth.

The path forward in a Zero Trust world is illuminated by a commitment to continuous learning and improvement. Organizations must remain agile, constantly reassessing their security posture in light of new threats and emerging technologies. This iterative process is best compared to a marathon rather than a sprint—a long-term commitment that requires endurance, resilience, and the willingness to adapt. Just as a marathon runner adjusts their pace based on the terrain and conditions, so too must organizations fine-tune their security strategies as the digital landscape evolves.

In this dynamic environment, collaboration and partnerships will be more important than ever. The vendor ecosystem supporting Zero Trust is vibrant and continuously evolving, offering specialized solutions that can be integrated into a unified security framework. Organizations that maintain strong relationships with their vendors, participate in industry consortia, and collaborate with regulatory bodies will be better positioned to adapt to the rapidly changing landscape. This network of partnerships is like a community of skilled artisans who work together to create a masterpiece—each contributor brings their unique expertise, and the result is a collective work of art that is far more resilient and innovative than any single effort could achieve.

As we close this journey, the message is clear: Zero Trust is not a static goal but an ongoing mission. It is a commitment to never take security for granted, to continually verify every access, and to remain ever-vigilant in the face of evolving threats. Organizations that embrace this mindset will not only protect their critical assets but will also foster a culture of resilience, innovation, and shared responsibility.

The road ahead is undoubtedly challenging. The digital landscape is fraught with uncertainty, and cyber adversaries are constantly developing new tactics to exploit vulnerabilities. However, by adopting a Zero Trust framework, organizations can transform these challenges into opportunities. Every breach, every near-miss, and every success is a stepping stone on the path to a more secure future. Just as a seasoned sailor learns to navigate stormy seas by studying every wave and adjusting their course, so too must cybersecurity professionals learn from every incident and adapt their strategies accordingly.

In essence, the journey to a Zero Trust world is a transformative process that reshapes not only our technical defenses but also our approach to risk, trust, and collaboration. It is a journey that demands unwavering commitment, innovative thinking, and a willingness to challenge conventional wisdom. As you move forward, remember that security is not an endpoint but a continuous process—a journey where every step is an opportunity to learn, improve, and fortify your defenses against the unpredictable tides of cyber threats.

The path forward in this Zero Trust world is paved with innovation, collaboration, and a relentless pursuit of excellence. It is a future where security is integrated into every facet of our digital lives, where every interaction is scrutinized, and where trust is continuously earned through rigorous, real-time verification. As organizations across the globe adopt and refine these principles, they lay the foundation for a digital ecosystem that is not only secure and resilient but also adaptive and forward-thinking—a world in which the only constant is the commitment to never trust by default, but always verify.

In closing, the promise of a Zero Trust world is both a challenge and an opportunity—a call to action for leaders, employees, vendors, and regulators alike. It is a journey that will require us to rethink our assumptions, innovate relentlessly, and work together to build a secure future that stands resilient against the evolving threats of tomorrow. The path forward is illuminated by the collective experience and wisdom shared in this book— a roadmap that, if followed with dedication and insight, will lead to a digital future where security is not just a safeguard, but a strategic asset that drives growth, inspires confidence, and underpins every facet of our interconnected world.

ABOUT THE AUTHOR

Bill Johns began his journey into the world of computing over 35 years ago, starting as a hobbyist building and upgrading computer hardware. His natural curiosity and technical aptitude soon led him to explore computer networks, and before long, he had built a large Bulletin Board System (BBS) that became a hub for early online communities. At the same time, Bill was applying his growing expertise to building corporate networks, helping businesses navigate the new landscape of interconnected systems.

When the internet began to take shape, Bill adapted his BBS to the online world, delving deep into internet protocols by reading RFCs (Request for Comments) and engaging with fellow tech pioneers on the Undernet, Dalnet, EfNet, and similar forums. His deep understanding of networks and security caught the attention of a major social networking platform, where, motivated by relentless attacks, he gained admin privileges on the network's servers through sheer skill and ingenuity. Faced with an ultimatum — explain how he did it and use his knowledge to defend the network, or face the consequences — Bill chose the high road. This decision launched him into several intense years of 24/7 live-fire hacker wars, where he was on the front lines defending critical systems from relentless attacks.

This battle-hardened experience opened the door to high-stakes contracts, including responding to the devastating effects of malware like Code Red and Nimda. Bill was brought in to help recover paralyzed networks that had been written off as lost causes — and he succeeded where others had failed. Once the dust settled from the early 2000s malware wars, Bill shifted his focus to building secure networks for U.S. Department of Defense (DoD) contractors, helping to protect national security infrastructure from emerging cyber threats.

Later in his career, Bill turned his expertise toward securing critical infrastructure, including IT and OT/ICS environments. His work spanned industries such as manufacturing, oil and gas, pharmaceuticals, automotive, water and wastewater systems, electrical power generation, and nuclear power plants. Over time, Bill's role expanded beyond technical problem-solving into the complex world of regulatory compliance and governance in the cybersecurity space. He became a trusted advisor in navigating the often-conflicting demands of security and regulation, helping industries strike the difficult balance between operational efficiency and meeting rigorous standards. Bill's accumulated knowledge and experience, stretching back to the early days of computer networking and the internet, provide a rare and invaluable perspective on the evolution of cybersecurity. His books reflect the hard-won lessons and insights gained from a career spent not just observing but actively shaping the development of secure digital systems — while also ensuring they meet the critical demands of regulatory oversight.